Du Pont Gardens *of the* Brandywine Valley

Du Pont Gardens *of the* Brandywine Valley

Photographs *by* Larry Lederman

Text by Marta McDowell

Foreword by Charles A. Birnbaum

CONTENTS

Preface

Hagley, Nemours, Winterthur, Mt. Cuba, and Longwood: these five gardens are among America's best. Considered together, as facets of one family's garden, they are unrivaled. I was introduced to the gardens in the spring of 2018 when I photographed at Winterthur to enhance its guidebook. I was then invited, in the winter of 2021, to photograph all five gardens and compile a book presenting their remarkable character and range. It was an irresistible opportunity, an honor, and an extraordinary pleasure.

I was drawn to the diversity and creativity of the gardens. Magnificently treed and planted woodlands lead to breathtaking vistas and meadowlands. Exquisitely designed Italian and French gardens provide the contrast of rigorous formal design. Showmanship is evident: there are beautiful allées and an inspired romantic ruin. Watercourses are numerous, running the gamut from streams and ponds and ingenious waterworks to the scenic Brandywine, which powered the original family mill. Such scope is a photographer's delight. Of equal importance was their history; each has its own notable story and character that continue to influence American horticulture.

Starting in early March 2021, I concluded that it would take most of the spring to get a good sense of the garden sites to be able to capture them. I decided I needed a year and a second spring to get all the images that I needed and wanted. Thus, my timeline was from March 2021 through June

RIGHT: Fountain jets animate Pierre S. du Pont's Italian Water Garden at Longwood Gardens.

OVERLEAF: An autumn sun casts angled shadows through the allée of maples (*Acer rubrum*) along the entry drive to Nemours Estate.

2022. In order to capture subtle changes, I determined to visit about every two weeks and spend two or three days photographing on each visit.

My experience with gardens and landscape design began many years before I was interested in photography. I'm infatuated with the beauty of trees and well-designed gardens. I took up the camera to explore and express my sense of wonder. From the outset of this project, I set out to do more than make a documentary record. The poet William Carlos Williams says that poets write "to give witness to splendor." My photographs give witness to splendor manifest in these gardens. Moreover, arresting moments capture the revelatory effects of seasonal and transient light. All the images share my wonder.

These photographs also seek to convey the immersive spell of being in the gardens. Frederick Law Olmsted describes his experience of viewing extraordinary landscapes in terms which he likens to listening to music. "Gradually and silently the charm carries over us: the beauty has entered our souls; we know not when and how." This immersive charm is visually present in these gardens, designed as natural havens to enthrall all visitors. No day was complete unless I was satisfied that I had captured that day's spell cast on me as I released the shutter.

Only then could I move on.

I edited my work as I went along. It was a provisional selection to keep track of what I had done. The decisive editing came at the end when I reviewed everything. To be included here, each photograph had to stand alone and also complement the others chosen in order to present a cohesive story. I am pleased and proud to present my selections in this book.

LARRY LEDERMAN

THE DU PONT LANDSCAPE LEGACY

PATRONS, ACCORDING TO THE LEARNED AND WORLDLY LANDSCAPE architect Laurie Olin, are generally motivated by three things: "piety, prestige, and pleasure." The concept of *patronage* can be traced back hundreds of years, if not longer. Just think of families such as the Medici in Renaissance Florence, who commissioned elaborate altarpieces for the city's famous churches and other great works of art. The Medici legacy also includes twelve villas and two gardens in Tuscany that are part of a World Heritage Site designated in 2013, among many other cultural treasures.

Olin also remarked at a 2012 conference about patronage convened by The Cultural Landscape Foundation: "Great landscapes, especially those that have endured for any length of time, invariably owe their character and value to the ideas, efforts, and vision of those that conceived of them and those who have brought them to realization." He added: "The person who conceives of a project, who has the desire for a particular landscape, garden, house, or estate, and who has the resources to pay for its design and construction is not the artist or designer. In some unusual instances these have been one in the same person—designer, patron, and builder."

Larry Lederman's evocative photography enables us to understand how "piety, prestige, and pleasure" were foundational to the patronage of American industrialists such as Pierre S. du Pont. Moreover, through the du Pont gardens now open to the public—five pioneering, unique, and

RIGHT: A corner of the South Garden at Mt. Cuba Center.

PAGE 22: Flower Garden Walk at Longwood Gardens.

PAGE 25: Sunken Garden at Nemours.

extraordinary places clustered in the Brandywine Valley—we gain a greater historical context for the du Pont family's patronage.

Indeed, we can evaluate and contextualize this more than two-hundred-year family legacy of patronage through the trajectory of one humble yet foundational Brandywine garden, a French potager, designed by the French-born American chemist and industrialist Éleuthère Irénée du Pont de Nemours (1771–1834), who immigrated to the United States in 1799. Nearly lost to the incremental ravages of time, by the mid-twentieth century, this rustic garden of pears, grapes, flowers, and vegetables was a grassed-over ghost of its former self. Enter Louise Evelina du Pont Crowninshield (1877–1958), whose work on the potager ushered in a new era of patronage. Indeed, it positioned the du Pont family's multi-generational landscape patronage on a continuum with historic European precedents and Industrialist-era families such as the Rockefellers, Fords, Vanderbilts, and a small number of others who founded and supported major cultural institutions in the late nineteenth century.

As Marta McDowell notes in the introductory essay: "After extensive garden archaeology in the late 1960s—among the first such studies in the United States—it [the potager] was rebuilt." It is this stewardship commitment to such pioneering innovations in landscape archaeology, and the resurrection and interpretation of this lost garden that is part of a family vision that embraces landscape design, horticultural innovation, landscape conservation, and historic preservation.

It's not by accident that the Louise du Pont Crowninshield Award annually bestowed by the National Trust for Historic Preservation is that organization's highest national honor. Consistent with its namesake's values, the award is "made with the greatest care and only when there is indisputable evidence of superlative achievement over time in the preservation and interpretation of our cultural, architectural or maritime heritage, including buildings, architecture, districts, archeology, cultural landscapes, and objects of significance in the history and culture of the United States."

The exceptionally high standards for the design and stewardship of the five gardens in this book range in type and style (e.g., Beaux-Arts, French, Italianate, Naturalistic), and scale (from humble to monumental). Taking them typologically and chronologically, this extraordinary twentieth-century American landscape patronage dynasty spans 1906 to 2001 and includes:

❋ Pierre S. du Pont's Longwood Gardens, whimsical and theatrical displays of water and horticultural exuberance in monumental fountains and conservatories.

❋ Alfred du Pont's Nemours, a grand Beaux-Arts interpretation of French neoclassical gardens that are simple and elegant, celebrated for its Carrère and Hastings architecture crowning terraced greenery.

❋ Henry Francis du Pont's Winterthur, a naturalized woodland garden that represents an extended collaboration between a patron/horticulturist and the landscape architect Marian Coffin.

❋ Louise du Pont Crowninshield and Francis Boardman Crowninshield's reconceived terraced ruins at Eleutherian Mills, a neoclassical Italianate stage set, draped in horticultural splendor and (to this day) little recognized for its interpretive innovation as a commemorative garden for the twelve workers who perished on site in an 1890 gunpowder explosion.

❋ Lammot du Pont Copeland and Pamela Cunningham Copeland's Mt. Cuba, with its traditional Country Place Era origins (with landscape architects Thomas Sears and Marian Coffin), ultimately becoming an enormously influential naturalistic native garden that Pamela Copeland watched over until her death in 2001.

The idea of landscape patronage in America is older than the profession of landscape architecture. In terms of our nation's parks and park systems, there is very often a great patron—Samuel Colt (Hartford), George Marston (San Diego), Andrew Mellon (Pittsburgh), and John D. Rockefeller Jr. (Cleveland, Ohio, and New York State), to name a few—supporting the efforts of the design team.

In addition to parks, significant estate landscapes of the Country Place era are now publicly accessible (and listed in the National Register of Historic Places), including Longwood Gardens, Nemours Estate, the Hagley Museum and Library's Crowninshield Garden, Winterthur Museum, Garden, and Library, and Mt. Cuba Center. These diverse estate landscapes were mostly executed between 1880s and 1930s, a time when the nation's millionaires were seeking ways to display their wealth. Drawing liberally, and at times indiscriminately, on Western European Renaissance traditions, as landscape historian Mac Griswold noted in *The Golden Age of American Gardens: Proud Owners Private Estates, 1890-1940*, "The struggle to become one of the elite took place at 'the country place' as much as in the ballroom or the boardroom, and thus a beautiful garden had the same social utility as good horses, a box at the opera, or magnificent dinner parties."

Another great landscape patron, Edward W. Bok (1863–1930), memorialized his personal philosophy for the bird sanctuary in Lake Wales, Florida, with its soaring carillon. The 250-acre landscape was designed by Frederick Law Olmsted Jr. and William Lyman Phillips of the Olmsted Brothers firm. Inscribed above the mantel in the south wall of the Founder's Room is Bok's exhortation: "Make your world a bit better or more beautiful because you have to live in it."

The du Pont family legacy of historically, culturally, ecologically significant gardens in the Brandywine Valley exemplify Bok's patronage philosophy. In 1906, when industrialist gentleman farmer Pierre S. du Pont purchased the agricultural land that would become Longwood Gardens, he noted that "the property was being denuded [of trees] for the benefit of the owner before the maturity of the debts incurred for its purchase." If it weren't for Pierre and the multi-generational du Pont family patronage that followed, more than these champion trees would have been lost.

The du Pont landscape patronage legacy today stands as a philanthropic model as well as a living witness to what can be achieved through a patron's vision and ambition. Laurie Olin, when probing the great works of landscape architecture that are also significant acts of patronage noted: "A fundamental reason for the need and involvement of patrons in landscape history is that landscape is a difficult medium in which to indulge one's vision. It requires enormous resources and time, as well as land—often, extensive tracts of real estate. Finally, most cultural landscapes involve careful planning and detailed development for the altering of land and drainage, infrastructure, and buildings involving engineering, planting, and myriad technical matters as well as issues of meaning, narrative, reference, and history—which render them among the most complex products a society can produce."

Larry Lederman's exquisite and encyclopedic photographic survey today clearly illustrates the full flowering of a collective vision. Much can be learned from the motivation and inspiration of the du Pont family and their unrivaled ambition, innovative acts of garden making, technological invention, and stewardship continuum all of which supported a truly unrivaled American design legacy.

CHARLES A. BIRNBAUM

THE DU PONT HERITAGE

 Horticulture and Stewardship

This is the story of five gardens. It is a story of a family—the du Ponts—the gardens they made, the gardens they preserved, and their place in the annals of American horticulture. At the same time, it is the story of land, a particular corner of the Mid-Atlantic Piedmont nestled along the shared border of Delaware and Pennsylvania, well-suited to plants. ❀ Together, these five gardens read as encyclopedic entries in the history of landscape design at home and abroad. Hagley, where the story began, has rebuilt the French-style potager planted by the first du Ponts who came to live, work, and garden along the Brandywine in 1802; more than a century later, one of their great-granddaughters and her spouse layered an Italianate garden atop the ruins of the original mill buildings. Winterthur was planned and planted by two du Ponts, father and son; over three generations of du Pont ownership, the

natural woodlands and agricultural lands evolved into a quintessential plantsman's garden in a naturalistic arts and crafts style. There is Longwood, with echoes of the great villa gardens of Quattrocento Italy and the pageantry of Versailles. Nemours takes a courtly bow to French Baroque gardens and curtsies to the English influences that infiltrated the Petit Trianon during the reign of Louis XVI. The newest garden of the five, Mt. Cuba, began rewilding the landscape well before the term was coined.

Yet as much as their elements can be traced to European antecedents, these are American gardens, each with unique traits reflecting their place and time. They are the gardens of inventors who interpreted a cultural diaspora of design influences for a North American landscape with new technologies, plants, and philosophies. They are gardens of ambition. Individually, their collections and displays are noteworthy; as a group they are stellar. It is no exaggeration to call the du Ponts the first family of American horticulture.

This volume celebrates that achievement through the work of Larry Lederman, whose extraordinary photographs capture the unique spirit of each place and create a compelling portrait of the unrivalled beauty of the Brandywine Valley.

ON NEW YEAR'S DAY 1950, more than six hundred du Pont descendants convened to dine among the plants and fountains in Pierre S. du Pont's vast conservatory at Longwood Gardens. Invitations had been issued, the menu prepared, and the program carefully planned for the Sunday afternoon gathering. It was part of a longstanding custom among the du Ponts. "New Year's calling" was and is a day of choreographed visits to relatives in and around Wilmington, marking the turn of each year and commemorating their collective lineage. But the formalities on the first of January that year–1950–denoted a particular anniversary, the sesquicentennial of the arrival of the du Ponts in the United States.

PREVIOUS PAGES: At Hagley, repurposed vessels from the saltpeter refinery mark a stairway in Louise du Pont and Francis Boardman Crowninshield's neoclassical garden.

OPPOSITE: Illuminated performances at the Main Fountain Garden have enthralled Longwood audiences since 1931.

ABOVE: Eleutherian Mills, c. 1950. The house overlooks the Crowninshield Garden, which is built into the hillside below.

Rewind to January 1, 1800, a new century, notable on its own. It was also the first page of a new chapter in the history of a family that would make its mark in industry and garden making. That day, a three-masted ship, the *American Eagle*, reached the waters off Newport, Rhode Island, after an arduous crossing from France. When its passengers disembarked, or likely staggered off, fourteen were members of the du Pont family: twenty-eight-year-old Éleuthère Irénée, his older brother Victor, their spouses and children, his father, Pierre Samuel, and stepmother, and a few in-laws. They were immigrants, having chosen to transplant themselves onto New World soil.

On the passport issued by the French Republic in 1799, Éleuthère Irénée du Pont–known to his intimates as Irénée, but whom we shall call E. I.–had noted as his profession *Botaniste*. "Botanist" was, perhaps, an avocation or future goal, as his botanical credentials were slim. With more accuracy, he might have called himself *Fabricant* or manufacturer, as he had skills in gunpowder production acquired at the Essonne mills under chemist Antoine Lavoisier. Or perhaps he might have written *Imprimeur* or printer, given solid experience in his father's Parisian publishing house. And then, it is possible that *Botaniste* was an obfuscation due to political unease between France and the United States, both still finding their way in newly won forms of government.

Still, E. I. was indisputably interested in plants. He had attended early morning lectures at the Jardin des Plantes in Paris, and he had packed his copious botany notes–two hundred neatly penned pages–in the baggage stowed on the *American Eagle*. Growing up at Bois-des-Fossés, his father's country estate, he had developed a naturalist's tendencies and a gardener's obsessions. After he settled in his American home, he would continue raising plants: productive plants to feed a large family and specimen trees to adorn the property.

ABOVE: Unknown artist, *American Eagle.* This ship, built in Massachusetts in 1795, brought members of the du Pont family from La Rochelle, France, to Newport, Rhode Island.

OPPOSITE: The manicured potager thrives in front of Eleutherian Mills.

OVERLEAF: Brandywine Creek.

The history of the du Ponts in America is often told as a story of the family and the firm, but theirs was not a rags-to-riches saga. The du Ponts had raised capital from investors in France, arriving in the United States with enough resources to establish credit, acquire land, and launch a business. E. I. du Pont was no dreamer. Serious and industrious, he brought with him a portfolio of manufacturing possibilities in America, including a potential market for gunpowder. Those opportunities brought the du Ponts to Delaware.

E. I. was soon engaged in building a mill and related works to produce black powder, used for gunpowder, ordnance, and explosives. For this new venture, he needed power. He chose a spot in the rural countryside, adjacent to Wilmington and not far from Philadelphia. Water and rock—hydrology and geology—were its industrial destiny.

Brandywine Creek, so central to the story of the du Ponts and their gardens, is not navigable. It rises in southeast Pennsylvania and flows across the Great Valley. Near the Delaware state line, it bumps into gneiss; over geologic time it had carved a channel that drops 120 feet in less than four miles. This is the Fall Line, where the Appalachian highlands of eastern North America descend to the coastal plain. The eight-mile stretch of fast-moving Brandywine water seemed tailor-made for powering mills: grain, paper, textiles, and, for the du Ponts, black powder. Vessels to move raw materials and finished product were plentiful in nearby Wilmington, with the confluence of the Christina, then, in turn, the broad Delaware River.

The du Pont family thrived. Their company grew to serve the seemingly limitless territory and economic potential of the United States in the early industrial era. Their product was in demand as the country expanded: supporting the mining industry in Pennsylvania and the Upper Midwest, clearing land, and building roads and railroads. The manufacturing wealth

generated by the company would fund a passion for gardens and gardening. That passion had its own sources, rooted in France.

Their patriarch, E. I.'s father, Pierre Samuel du Pont de Nemours, had been a political economist. Ennobled by Louis XVI, he had represented Nemours, an Île-de-France commune, in the Estates General of 1789. "Land and water are the sole sources of wealth," he once wrote, promoting a rural social order anchored in cultivating the land. His agrarian philosophy aligned with Thomas Jefferson's, his friend and correspondent. "Bon

LEFT: The Hagley Visitor Center was built in 1812 as a textile mill.

ABOVE: A large bank barn was among the first buildings E. I. du Pont constructed at Eleutherian Mills.

ABOVE: Holstein herd at Winterthur, 1930s.

OPPOSITE: A chorus of tulips, fritillaries, and daffodils harmonize in this exuberance of spring bulbs along Longwood's Flower Garden Walk.

OVERLEAF: Colonel Henry du Pont and his son Henry Francis used the East Barn complex for livestock, and Winterthur continues the agriculture tradition.

Papa" had encouraged his children to adopt a utopian lifestyle in America, a communal, agricultural approach; perhaps, he suggested, they might call it "Pontiana." Manufacturing had not been part of that plan, though it became a financial reality. Du Pont de Nemours and his wife returned to France in 1802, but his influence on his children persisted.

After the powder works, E. I. turned his attention to constructing the monumental stone barn still gracing the grounds. Then he worked on the residences. He built his family home close to the barn and directly above the mill. He and his wife, his in-laws, and later their offspring, built an expanding residential compound dotted around the property. There were comfortable if modest houses for the extended family, dormitories and cottages for workers, and a non-denominational Sunday school for their children. There was an office for management and administration, a company store with fair pricing, a credit union, and a regular daily transport to and from downtown Wilmington. The du Pont women taught the children of workers in schools built on the grounds. And E. I. planted a garden.

The du Ponts were a group with cosmopolitan tastes and varied accomplishments. They enjoyed music, art, literature, and natural history. E. I. and his sons improved the garden and grounds, directed farm operations, and joined local agricultural societies. The women added flowers to the garden, tended potted plants, and collected, pressed, and mounted botanical specimens for their herbarium collections. Gardeners and laborers provided the regular maintenance. In the du Pont cemetery, their first longtime gardener, John Prevost, is interred in one of the few non-family plots.

The company prospered as decades progressed, and descendants of the du Ponts multiplied. They spread across the United States, though many stayed nearby. Later generations acquired more and larger adjacent parcels of land around the valley of the Brandywine. A map of the area

from the 1920s through the 1940s shows nearly the entire region owned by members of the family.

As E. I. du Pont had seen to barn and fields at Eleutherian Mills, many of the Brandywine du Ponts continued to engage in agriculture. Nemours had its Blue Ball Dairy and Longwood its Webb Barn. At the September 1920 Delaware State Fair, Winterthur swept most of the prizes in the Holstein-Friesian cattle competition. But more than farms, the du Ponts became known for their gardens.

The greatest generation of du Pont garden makers were great-grandchildren or, in one case, a great-great-grandchild of the company's founder, E. I. du Pont. Five of them—Henry Francis, Pierre Samuel, Alfred Irénée, Louise du Pont Crowninshield, and Lammot du Pont Copeland—created the five gardens in this book. Their adult lives converged with a trend in grand residential landscapes: the Country Place Era, what has been called the Golden Age of American Gardens.

They made family gardens for family homes. Beauty, yes, but also utility. The du Ponts enjoyed their gardens. Scrapbooks, photograph albums, and home movies chronicle their varied uses: du Ponts cutting flowers, picnicking, playing with children, swimming, entertaining, and celebrating every sort of event. Their outdoor spaces were extensions of the relaxed, generally understated style of the clan.

The du Ponts were not inclined to build palace-like mansions. But they did buy land. Theirs was horticulture at a gargantuan scale; Winterthur has its own zip code and had its own train station. These gardens and their managed grounds add up to more than 3,500 acres today.

If the three criteria for success of any garden are money, manure, and maintenance, the du Pont budgets amply allowed for all three. They funded the salaries of head gardeners, horticulturists, grounds staff, masons, and, where necessary, designers. They enabled acquisitions of fountains,

architectural features, and statuary. The du Ponts ordered so many plants in such numbers that they were courted by the American nursery industry for much of the twentieth century.

Among these du Pont gardeners, competitive spirit—mostly friendly—was inevitable. To some degree, each specialized. Yet there were commonalities. They had geographic proximity, located within a ten-mile radius. They shared the rolling countryside of the Brandywine Valley, which also attracted artists, notably the Wyeths. The location is far enough south to enjoy benign temperatures and a broad plant palette. The soil is rich and the water plentiful.

As if in acknowledgment of the family history of waterpower, these du Ponts made creative, innovative use of water features. At Hagley, a recreation of E. I.'s early nineteenth-century pump adorns the potager. Frank and Louise Crowninshield brought the Brandywine itself into their garden scheme. Pierre and Alfred both were capable hydraulic engineers: Longwood is famous for its fountains; Nemours's main axis is a series of water features powered by Alfred's innovative system. Winterthur's natural streams wind through its gardens, while the man-made pools at Mt. Cuba blend seamlessly into its designed woodland.

During the 1920s, Charles Sprague Sargent, the first director of the Arnold Arboretum and dean of American horticulture at the time, christened a hybrid horse chestnut (*Aesculus* x *dupontii*) in the family's honor. In a 1924 issue of the Arboretum journal, Sargent credited the du Ponts with making "the neighborhood of Wilmington, Delaware, one of the chief centers of horticulture in America."

That Sargent chose to name a tree for the du Ponts is especially apt, as the history of the region could be told through its trees. It is a geographical sweet spot for arboreal growth. Well before the du Ponts began acquiring the land, great trees had grown. The Lenape people had inhabited

OPPOSITE: Clenny Run, a Brandywine tributary, winds through Winterthur's garden and pastures.

ABOVE: The reconstruction of the 1817 pump at Hagley was guided by a sketch, c. 1870, by architect Theophilus P. Chandler.

OVERLEAF: The historic trees in Peirce's Park at Longwood are graced with an underplanting of rhododendron, bottlebrush buckeye (*Aesculus parviflora*), geophytes, and ferns.

the forests for at least ten thousand years. There they hunted, gathered plants, and fished in the streams, creeks, and rivers that comprise the watershed of what is now called the Delaware River. Settlers cleared land for farming; some of them planted new trees for practical, intellectual, and aesthetic reasons.

Since then, the du Ponts, their gardeners, and the horticulturists at the public gardens they endowed have planted many, many more. In both arboriculture—the care of ornamental trees—and silviculture—the care of forest trees—these gardens excel. The countless young trees they are planting today will grow into tomorrow's forest canopy.

Their mature trees are a presence. In Delaware's "Big Tree" survey, more than two dozen specimens at Hagley, Mt. Cuba, Nemours, and Winterthur have made the count. Longwood Gardens has more than sixty Pennsylvania state champions, the highest concentration anywhere in the Commonwealth. The national champion dawn redwood (*Metasequoia glyptostroboides*) grows there. These behemoths are living witnesses to history.

Over time, each owner chose to transform their properties from private residences to non-profit institutions, opening their homes, gardens, and grounds to the public. This went beyond pride of place. Providing for the common good was the norm among the du Ponts. Though many of them were engaged in manufacturing, du Ponts also served in the military, held public office, and led charities. Many have focused on the preservation of historic sites. Locals among the staff at the gardens today remember attending du Pont schools, recuperating at du Pont hospitals, and playing in parkland donated by this generous family. As the pressure of expansion from Philadelphia and Wilmington increased in the region, du Ponts became leaders in land conservation, treasured as open space and environmental buffer zones. It is a legacy they helped ensure through the public gardens they launched.

All five gardens are members of the American Public Gardens Association, of which Longwood was one of the founding members in 1940. As a network of professionals in the field of public horticulture, the Association provides a platform for action and advocacy.

It has spearheaded the Plant Collections Network to help safeguard the diversity of global flora. Both Longwood and Mt. Cuba are accredited participants, the former for waterlilies (*Nymphaea*) and the latter for *Trillium* and *Hexastylis*, diminutive, charming relatives of gingers. As qualified curators for key national plant collections, they will protect these unique genera for future gardeners, scientists, and the world.

As public institutions, the five gardens look to the future of horticulture and conservation through education. They offer courses of study, public lectures, tours, internships, and family programs, varying according to their individual missions. The school and fellowship programs at Longwood supply qualified professionals to staff and lead botanic gardens nationwide.

This book portrays a quintet of garden masterpieces united by the horticultural legacy of the du Ponts. Hagley, Winterthur, Nemours, Mt. Cuba, Longwood. While they are five separate institutions, they are closely linked because, in a deep sense, they are all related. Family members created them and continue to support them. Larry Lederman illuminates their beauty, their uniqueness, and their common threads through the art of photography.

In early spring, Quaker ladies (*Houstonia caerulea*) carpet the acidic soil along the West Slope Path at Mt. Cuba Center.

GARDENS LOST AND FOUND

 Hagley Museum and Library

AS SOON AS HE ARRIVED IN THE BRANDYWINE VALLEY, ÉLEUTHÈRE Irénée du Pont saw the need for a garden on the property he would call Eleutherian Mills. He could picture it, productive and rich, stretching up the slope in front of the site of his new home. In an August 1803 letter to Louis Lelieur, a friend in France, he wrote. "When I began building my establishment here, it was like settling in the back country, no road, no decent house, no garden." He added, "Being without a garden was the greatest deprivation; and it is the first thing that occupied my time." ❋ In response, Lelieur arranged for an order of seeds and nursery plants for his former compatriot. Any garden enthusiast can imagine E. I. du Pont's thrill when the wooden cases arrived from Bordeaux the following spring. From the shipment, he unpacked over two hundred juvenile fruit, nut, and

46

ornamental trees. There were grapevines, rooted cuttings of tarragon, raspberry canes, and many vegetable seeds. Flowers were not neglected, with rosebushes and divisions of lavender. These were living reminders of his birthplace, ready to grow in his adopted home.

The design would be French, as well as the plant material. Characteristic symmetry ruled. Created in the first years of the nineteenth century, it harkened back to the seventeenth. The potager was balanced and controlled, a study in geometry, a sanctuary of sense. Numbered among its predecessors are Louis XIV's *potager du roi* at Versailles, created by the king of classical French landscape designers, André Le Nôtre.

In a large rectangle about an acre in extent, du Pont laid out his garden in a manner both practical and pleasing to his ordered tastes. Bisected by neat paths and subdivided into smaller rectangles and squares, there was ample room for vegetables and small fruits in tidy rows, rosebushes, and a cutting bed for flowers. Meticulously pruned dwarf fruit trees added height without casting too much shade. Over the years, the garden doubled in size. Workers added arbors for grapes and hops. A toolhouse and pump were practical additions. Steps and a curving stone wall faced the house for a stylish entry. Cold frames and a small greenhouse extended the growing season.

Trees held their own attraction. E. I. du Pont shared an enthusiasm for arboriculture with many of his contemporaries. He wrote impassioned letters about the potential of American plant introductions, particularly trees, to French government officials. In addition to an orchard, du Pont and, later, his children planted trees at Eleutherian Mills, some as specimens and many in allées, those matched pairs of trees flanking roads and vistas in French chateaux.

Allées of sweet gum and oak lined the carriage road. The road led on axis to the front door of the house, stucco over stone, that E. I. du Pont

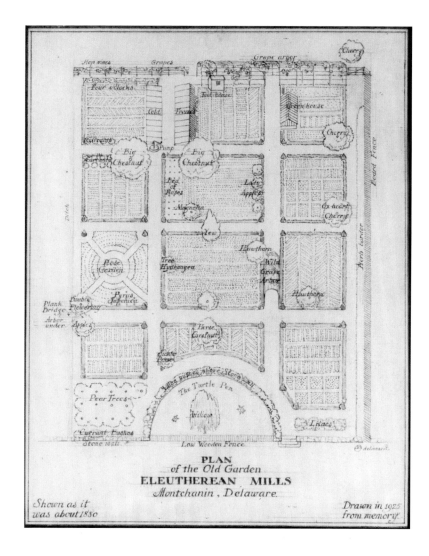

PREVIOUS PAGES: A mature sweet gum allée lines the original carriage drive and frames the entrance of Eleutherian Mills.

OPPOSITE: The horticulturists at Hagley employ traditional pruning and espalier techniques to manage the fruit trees in the E. I. du Pont Garden.

ABOVE: *Plan of the Old Garden at Eleutherean Mills, shown as it was about 1880,* drawn from memory by Victorine E. du Pont Foster, 1925.

PREVIOUS PAGES: Sweet gum
(*Liquidambar styraciflua*)
form a canopied allée
each summer.

ABOVE: Eleutherian Mills,
c. 1928, after the circular
entrance drive was installed.

RIGHT: For many years the
du Ponts ran their company
from a small stone office
building next to the house.

OVERLEAF: The terrace overlooks
the Crowninshield Garden and
the original powder works.

built. The family moved into the center portion, its first modest phase, in
1803. Forty years later, E. I.'s son Henry added wings on either side as both
family and business flourished.

Architecturally, the house is an exploration of symmetry with tall,
double-hung windows, a fanlight over the main door, and a gabled roof
pierced by three high dormers. Meticulously trained wisteria softens the
facade, though originally the wrought-iron back porch, reminiscent of the
French Quarter in New Orleans, ornamented the front of the house. To
the back there was, and still is, a fine prospect of the Brandywine. It was a
convenient overlook for a family whose livelihood depended on the manu-
factory in the line of sight.

The du Ponts at Eleutherian Mills shared the dangers of powder production with their employees. Despite safety measures, there were accidents. After a horrific explosion in 1890—twelve were killed and many injured—the du Pont family left the original homestead. Two years later, the house became headquarters for the Brandywine Club, a membership organization for employees. In 1921, when the DuPont Company closed operations at Eleutherian Mills and offered the property to interested family members, Henry Algernon du Pont decided to buy it for his married daughter Louise.

In 1938 Russian-born artist Nicolas de Molas took up brushes and canvas along the Brandywine Creek at the home of Frank and Louise du Pont Crowninshield. They were not his first society commission. He had painted estate and family portraits for names like Astor and Belin. De Molas's 1938 subject was specific: the Crowninshields and their dogs, posed in the terraced neoclassical garden built on the foundations of the original, by then defunct, du Pont powder works. It was romanticism atop industrialization like a metaphor writ large.

For Louise, Eleutherian Mills had been a fine gift from her father. It was his birthplace, and she cherished memories of visiting her grandparents there. She and her husband, Francis Boardman "Frank" Crowninshield, maintained their principal household in Boston, as well as a place in Marblehead, Massachusetts, for summer and another in Boca Grande, Florida, for winter. They were happy to have a home for spring and fall visits to her extensive Delaware family to round out the year.

Before his daughter and son-in-law took possession in 1925, Henry Algernon du Pont had readied the property. He hired an architect and renovated the interior of the house. Under his direction, contractors razed the closest mill buildings in preparation for extending the garden between the house and the Brandywine.

OPPOSITE: The layout of the terraced rooms in the Crowninshield Garden is most legible in winter and early spring.

ABOVE: Nicolas de Molas, *Frank and Louise du Pont Crowninshield in their Garden at Eleutherian Mills*, 1938.

While Louise, like her younger brother, Henry Francis du Pont, was a friend of landscape architect Marian Coffin, the Crowninshields did not engage a professional garden designer for Eleutherian Mills. They conceived their own whimsical plan and hired local craftsmen. The garden would be artifice, an invented Pompeii, a fictional ruin unearthed for modern eyes, no doubt inspired by their travels to Europe. On top of the manufacturing foundations, they added faux Italian elements. Brick, mortar, mosaic, and marble became reflecting pools, colonnades, and arches. A pool house took the form of a peristyle temple. Frank Crowninshield took

LEFT: Foundations of the original mill buildings on the banks of the Brandywine.

ABOVE: *Piping Boy*, a patinated bronze sculpture by Phil Shelton Sears, has stood at the edge of the Crowninshields' swimming pool since the 1920s.

 61

the lead in planning and managing the project. For one of his birthday parties, a guest wrote an alphabet poem in his honor; "G" was for "the Garden that hangs on the hill/Which Frank to develop has toiled with a will."

Frank and Louise repurposed industrial artifacts as garden elements. Great kettles, once used for refining saltpeter as part of the powder manufacturing process, became decorative urns mounted on pedestals. The mill wheel was absorbed into the design, and the Brandywine millrace stood in for an ornamental canal.

Mythological elements abounded: Medusa's head, lions, a mosaic swan recalling Leda and Zeus. Plentiful statuary—mostly modern versions of Greco-Roman deities—populated their garden creation. Borrowing was not limited to the classical realm. An arcade of twisted columns was patterned after the thirteenth-century cloister in St. Paul's Outside the Walls in Rome.

ABOVE: Replica of the Frascati Gate installed by Francis Boardman Crowninshield in the Colonnade Garden, 1935.

RIGHT: Flowering cherries (*Prunus serrulata*) and rhododendron are reminders of the original Shrub Terrace that grew beyond the gate.

ABOVE: Arched opening to the Mosaic Terrace, c. 1950.

OPPOSITE: Craftsmen set the floor mosaics directly over photographic enlargements of original Roman designs to ensure authenticity.

Correspondence and invoices addressed to Mrs. Frank Crowninshield indicate Louise as the principal in planting. Her design scheme was abundance with a touch of formality. Columnar cedars provided vertical accents. Boxwoods, rather than being tightly pruned, were allowed to loosen into graceful, rounded mounds. Flowering trees and shrubs shaded stone paths. Terraces frothed with dry garden plants. Emphasis was on spring bloom and fall color, when the couple would be in residence. Narcissus, tulips, azaleas, and magnolias dominated the early months of the year; late gladiolas and chrysanthemums for autumn. She once wrote, "The charm of the art of gardening lies in trying to place each flower as perfectly as possible in an effort to make a growing picture." On occasion, Pierre S. du Pont, in gardening attire, would stop by from Longwood to "fiddle in [his] cousin's garden."

The Crowninshields' garden was tour worthy. On May 16, 1929, Louise, along with brother Henry and cousin Pierre, opened their gardens to the thousand participants of the Garden Club of America's annual meeting. She stayed involved in Club activities wherever they were in residence, whether Massachusetts, Florida, or Delaware.

At the Club's headquarters on East 60th Street in New York City, the main conference room is the Crowninshield Room. Louise was a force in the organization and served in executive positions including national vice president. She was also a force to be reckoned with. In the 1920s and 1930s, Crowninshield lobbied officials from the Departments of Agriculture and Commerce, members of Congress, and President Harding to lift quarantine restrictions on Dutch bulbs. A substantial presence, known for her wit and flamboyant attire, she and her committee succeeded after a long battle.

Louise was also a dedicated preservationist. She was among the founding trustees of the National Trust for Historic Preservation; its highest award is named in her honor. She ensured the house at Eleutherian Mills, its collection of family memorabilia and American antiques, its gardens and

LEFT: Potted agaves once grew above the columns and along the balustrade, which enclosed a garden of boxwood knot beds.

ABOVE: Reflecting Pool, c. 1950.

OVERLEAF: Cabbages, poppies (*Papaver orientale*), and artichokes grow in the burgeoning summer potager. According to family tradition, E. I. du Pont introduced the poppy to America with seeds from the Jardin des Plantes in Paris.

67

grounds, and the remains of the powder works would be stewarded after her death. With her blessing, the Eleutherian Mills Historical Library was built on land near her home. It was dedicated in 1961, three years after her death.

Eleutherian Mills, a National Historic Landmark, is now under the umbrella of Hagley Museum and Library. The organization took its name from an adjacent property downstream on the Brandywine; E. I. du Pont had purchased it in 1813 to expand operations.

THE DU PONTS CREATED TWO distinct and distinctive gardens at Eleutherian Mills. Built more than a century apart, they are rare examples in American landscape history. One would be hard-pressed to find their equal anywhere on this side of the Atlantic, though at present they are in very different states of restoration.

By the mid-twentieth century, the potager had long been grassed over. After extensive garden archaeology in the late 1960s—among the first such studies in the United States—it was rebuilt. It continues to be beautifully maintained. Espaliered fruit grows along the fence of a once-again productive garden. There are heirloom varieties of cut flowers and vegetables, from the peas and salad greens of spring to the hard squash gathered after the last frost. Harvests are donated to Wilmington food pantries. The orchard grows fifty heritage varieties of apple, pear, peach, plum, and cherry trees, and a recent collaboration with Wilmington Brew Works puts part of its yield to good use.

Not far from the potager and the main allée is a tenacious Osage orange (*Maclura pomifera*), dating to the original du Pont period. It is a curious tree, an ancient species native to Texas and noted for its hard wood, though the fruits are inedible. This specimen was designated as a national champion for its age and size in 2011, only to be felled by the winds of a tornado nine years later. A persistent plant, it is resprouting from its giant roots.

ABOVE AND RIGHT: In spring Virginia bluebells (*Mertensia virginica*), mayapples (*Podophyllum peltatum*), and daffodils fill in the hillside of the Crowninshield Garden while redbuds (*Cercis canadensis*) and dogwoods bloom on the terraces.

Sadly, especially given Louise du Pont Crowninshield's commitment to historic preservation, the hillside garden is inaccessible at present. Its steps and terraces—precarious even when new—are now unsafe. Snake-haired Medusa looks out onto a silent, secret garden, still filled with the columns, pools, and grottoes built by Frank Crowninshield over industrial relics of the earlier du Ponts. In early spring, bulbs and flowering trees offer clues to Louise's plantings. There is romance here, and potential for immense interest from landscape architects, historians, and visitors. Like the old Osage orange, it is a garden poised to resprout from its roots.

LEFT: A sugar maple (*Acer saccharum*) in bloom on the banks of the Brandywine just beyond the Crowninshield Garden.

OVERLEAF: Stone structures and a mill wheel along the Brandywine are tangible reminders of the du Pont family's manufacturing past.

73

On a summer day, the Brandywine flows quietly through managed woodlands and alongside historic architecture at Hagley.

A Collector's Garden

 Winterthur Museum, Garden, and Library

In 1928, the year after he had inherited Winterthur, the almost fifty-year-old Henry Francis du Pont approached longtime friend Marian Coffin, with whom he shared a love of plants. While he was at Harvard, Coffin was a special student in landscape design at the Massachusetts Institute of Technology, and they toured European gardens together after graduation, properly chaperoned by her mother. ✳ Coffin had since become an experienced professional, underscored by her designation as a Fellow of the American Society of Landscape Architects. "Dear Marian," he wrote in his letter, "I am thinking of putting an addition to this house and changing the front door to an entirely different place, which means rearranging the grounds at the back of the house towards the garden."

This was a magnificent understatement, as what an addition it would be, more than tripling the size of his fifty-room childhood home. His plan was not residential, but curatorial. He needed space to hold his growing collection of American antiques—furniture, decorative arts, architectural features—eventually numbering in the tens of thousands of items, displayed in period settings that doubled as the family's living quarters. In his letter to Coffin, he declared, "I will want the garden to be finished with the house, so I would like to have immediate concentration of thought upon it."

This was grand hyperbole, as du Pont, a superb plantsman, was never finished. From his college days until his death in 1969, he built and

improved the gardens at Winterthur. He would create a naturalistic land-scaped garden unrivaled in North America, and perhaps the world.

In his horticultural interests, Henry Francis du Pont followed in his parents' footsteps. His mother loved roses, and he developed a passion for flowers. His father would sometimes quiz Harry, as he was known to family and close friends, and his older sister Louise on the scientific names of plants before they sat down to dinner. From boarding school at Groton, Harry's letters were packed with questions about the estate's plants and plantings.

Henry Francis du Pont had an intimate connection to Winterthur. His love of the land had been, in the words of his daughter, "bred in the bone." Winterthur has quirks of topography, part steep, part moist with springs. This had saved pockets of forest from the plow, though it had been logged. As early as the 1830s, a visitor had described its second growth woodlands as "wild as the mountains of Virginia." Its hills and dales, its natural streams, give the landscape its signature, its fluidity.

Henry and Louise were raised surrounded by Winterthur's meadows and mature trees. Their father, Henry Algernon du Pont, prized its arboreal heritage. He also added to it, developing it as a private arboretum. At his request, Charles Sprague Sargent, director of the Arnold Arboretum, came to consult and document the estate's tree species. Today, the prized tree collection continues to lend heft to Winterthur's gardens and grounds.

The property had been in the family since 1810. E. I. du Pont bought 181 acres of what is now Winterthur for sheep breeding. He called it "Merino Farm," noting it was "only a mile" from his house at Eleutherian Mills, "in a very pretty location." Thirty years later, his daughter, Evelina du Pont Bidermann, and son-in-law re-christened it Winterthur, after his ancestral home in Switzerland. Ownership passed briefly to their son, then to three Henry du Ponts in succession, grandfather, father, and son: first

LEFT: Meadow and specimen trees below Oak Hill blend with greensward and sky in a bucolic autumn vista.

OVERLEAF, ABOVE LEFT: The Latimeria gates beckon visitors through an arch of Wilson pearlbush (*Exochorda giraldii* var. *wilsonii*) to the curving path into the Pinetum.

OVERLEAF, BELOW LEFT: A specimen rhododendron (*Rhododendron oreodoxa* var. *fargesii*) in a dense underplanting of Italian windflower (*Anemone apennina*) adds visual interest in the layered woodland garden.

OVERLEAF, RIGHT: Azalea Woods is a blooming carpet of Italian windflower, great white trillium (*T. grandiflorum*), and Virginia bluebells (*Mertensia virginica*).

"Boss Henry," then Henry Algernon, a.k.a. "The Colonel," and finally to Henry Francis du Pont. They would enlarge Winterthur to more than two thousand acres.

Unlike most of his du Pont male cousins, who majored in engineering, Henry Francis pursued a course of study at Bussey Institution, Harvard's school of agriculture and horticulture. Boston was the nexus of the botanical world at the turn of the twentieth century when Henry arrived. He talked to plantsmen, kept what would become a lifelong gardening notebook, and, according to family lore, worked part-time at a local nursery, much to the astonishment of his parents.

While he was in college, Winterthur continued to occupy his thoughts. He began to plant narcissus in quantity along the streambank in those years, directing the estate's gardeners to put in bulbs en masse, grouped by single species or variety. He had been introduced to this wild garden effect, a tenet of British garden authorities William Robinson and Gertrude Jekyll, in his Harvard course on hardy herbaceous perennials. At Winterthur, this signaled the start of "bank to bend," what would become March Bank, stretching to Magnolia Bend. Not long after his return from Cambridge, his father—a newly elected U. S. Senator—turned over management of Winterthur's greenhouses, gardens, and grounds to his son.

So authorized, Henry Francis du Pont did not waste time. The first year, 1909, he ordered twenty-nine thousand spring-flowering bulbs for the gardeners to install; another thirty-nine thousand went in the next. He learned to make the drifts look natural by outlining planting areas with irregular branches gathered from the woods. By 1914 visitors were calling it "the garden of Mr. Harry du Pont," omitting mention of the Colonel. After a visit that May, J. P. Morgan's wife, Jessie, wrote, "We shall long remember the feast of flowers! The most beautiful combination of colors, both indoors and out."

RIGHT: The April daffodil display along the entry drive echoes Henry Francis du Pont's signature sweeps of bulbs.

OVERLEAF: Sun filters through the emerging leaf canopy to highlight colors in Azalea Woods.

Indoors and out. Colors and patterns inside the house—floral arrangements, fabrics, and china—matched the garden's displays. This was no accident. Henry Francis du Pont orchestrated both garden and home decor, a task he had taken on after his mother died in 1903. He coordinated interior with exterior, adjusting with the season. In the 1920s, he had become smitten with American decorative arts. The antiques he placed in the garden—statuary, sundials, summerhouses—echoed the choice furnishings he collected for the house.

He had augmented his academic education with garden travel. In the United States, he attended flower shows, sought out nurseries, and visited gardens, public and private. He crossed the Atlantic regularly with family and friends. The gardens of British and continental country houses opened their gates to his horticultural enthusiasms. They influenced Winterthur in turn. After a father-son visit to Dropmore, the Buckinghamshire estate built for Lord Grenville, the two Henry du Ponts returned to Delaware fired with excitement about conifers. Thus, the Pinetum was born.

Chestnut blight ravaged American forests in the early years of the twentieth century, and Winterthur had not been immune. Alert to new plant possibilities, Henry Francis spotted a small group of new azaleas at one of his favorite nurseries, Cottage Gardens on Long Island. The proprietor had purchased the seventeen gold-medal winning "Kurume hybrids" from the Domoto Nursery in California. The plants had been exhibited by the Akashi Kourakuen Nursery at San Francisco's 1915 Panama-Pacific Exposition. Domoto snapped them up, likely the first commercially available specimens in the Western Hemisphere. Their vigor, bloom, and glossy leaves inspired him. In the gaps left by Winterthur's vanished chestnuts, they thrived. His capable staff, led by a Scottish head gardener, propagated hundreds more. From year to year,

ABOVE: Flowering quince delighted Henry Francis du Pont, and Quince Walk continues to delight visitors each April.

OPPOSITE: Crabapples between the Sundial Garden and the Pinetum.

OVERLEAF, LEFT: Winterthur's extensive trails offer views of woodland, meadow, and farm on its nearly one thousand preserved acres.

OVERLEAF, RIGHT: Native grasses and forbs are maintained in the upland meadows with annual haying.

du Pont fine-tuned the color balance, sometimes relocating full-sized shrubs in bloom. His original azalea planting eventually covered eight acres. To wander Azalea Woods in spring is to step into an Impressionist painting and amble through vibrant, living artistry.

The landscape at Winterthur was his horticultural canvas. His plant palette grew exponentially, with massive orders from the best nurseries and relationships with top botanical gardens. Collecting was in his nature. "It takes a sack of money to collect the way Harry du Pont has done," a friend once commented. "But it also takes a lot more than money. It takes a sure eye for beauty, a perfect sense of balance, and an incredible amount of work." Winterthur was Henry Francis du Pont's muse and his horticultural laboratory.

He extended and updated the greenhouse range. The staff grew cut flowers and houseplants for indoor display, fruits and vegetables for the table, and plant material for the grounds. In nearby trial beds, du Pont and his team tested new species and compared varieties, assessing labeled specimens to choose the best for the gardens.

He consulted with the top echelon of plant professionals. With questions about herbaceous plants, du Pont corresponded with luminaries such as Gertrude Jekyll at Munstead Wood and Ellen Willmott at Warley Place. For a peony border, he consulted with Dr. A. P. Saunders and J. Franklin Styer, preeminent American hybridizers. To supplement his azalea and rhododendron collection, he worked with Charles Dexter and Joseph Gable. For daylilies, he turned to Dr. A. B. Stout at the New York Botanical Garden. And he always maintained a close relationship with Charles Sprague Sargent and his successors at the Arnold Arboretum.

Each year, du Pont recorded dates and successive waves of bloom at Winterthur, a practice he carried on for a half century. It was a job that grew with his garden. Collection followed collection. Acquisitions of

flowering quince cultivars became *Chaenomeles* Walk; a trial of *Corylopsis* grew into Winterhazel Walk. More magnolias joined those his father had cultivated. Ornamental cherries burst into pink and white extravagance in April. Peonies unfurled in May, surrounded by arcs of lilac and beauty bush (*Kolkwitzia amabilis*). He amended the display in Azalea Woods, adding native dogwood as an understory and Virginia and Spanish bluebells (*Mertensia virginica* and *Hyacinthoides hispanica*) for a carpet of blue. His horticultural tastes were catholic.

Yet as much as Winterthur is a flower garden, it is also an expression of the pastoral. Its vistas of park and farmland echo the eighteenth-century

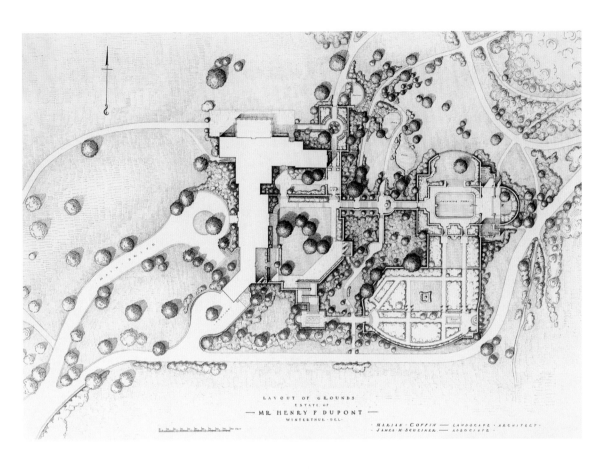

LAYOUT OF GROUNDS
ESTATE OF
— MR. HENRY F DUPONT —
WINTERTHUR·DEL·

· MARIAN · COFFIN — LANDSCAPE · ARCHITECT ·
· JAMES M SCHEINER — ASSOCIATE ·

English landscape movement of William Kent and Capability Brown and the American designs of Frederick Law Olmsted. It is bucolic and was, at the time, agrarian.

On passports and legal documents, Henry Francis du Pont would sometimes write in "farmer" for his occupation. When he told his father of his plans to start a dairy, the Colonel observed that it would cost less than a yacht and do more for humanity. Henry Francis du Pont honored the farming traditions of his forebears, overlaid with modern, scientific techniques.

LEFT: An elegant armillary sphere is the focal point of the Sundial Garden.

ABOVE: Marian Coffin's plan of the garden and grounds, c. 1930.

OVERLEAF: Henry Francis du Pont created a showcase of herbaceous and tree peonies for the Peony Garden starting in the 1940s.

built a model dairy barn as well as a prize-winning herd. Winterthur Farms supplied milk, meat, eggs, and produce for family and staff, and surplus to sell in the Wilmington area.

Marian Coffin's work at Winterthur began in 1928 with du Pont's grand addition to the house. It would evolve into the largest commission of her career, and his referrals would gain her many other clients. Her first effort was to marry the enormous residence to the site. The main axis visually connects the primary bedroom suite with a grand outdoor staircase set among symmetrical terraces. It leads to a rectangular water feature that doubled, as in so many du Pont gardens, as the family swimming pool. Her transition to less formal areas like March Bank were smooth. Henry Francis's wife, Ruth Wales du Pont, appreciated the results. "The place looks too beautiful for words," she wrote her mother in April 1931. "Marian has done a superlative job—she sure has the eye and the ability. . . She has managed house & grounds into a perfect unit."

Over the years, Coffin provided technical expertise for the Sundial Garden and the Box Scroll Garden among others, but Winterthur always remained Henry Francis du Pont's personal project. For that reason, it retained a cohesive sense of place. Walking Winterthur is both intimate and expansive. Through sunlight and shadow, it blends vistas and focal points with plants of horticultural merit. Its composition flatters nature. It flows.

By the 1930s, du Pont was already planning for Winterthur's future as a museum and public garden. In a memorandum to his executors, he wrote, "I sincerely hope . . . that the gardens and grounds will of themselves be a country place museum where visitors may enjoy as I have, not only the flowers, trees and shrubs, but also the sunlit meadows, shady wood paths, and the peace and great calm of a country place which has been loved and taken care of for three generations." Winterthur was his masterpiece.

ABOVE AND RIGHT: Marian Coffin designed the family's swimming pool, now converted to a Reflecting Pool, as part of her plan for the property. In spring, flowering azaleas, viburnums, and dogwoods shimmer on the surface of the water.

Despite his accomplishments, he was a shy man, a man of few words. When the residence with its treasures of American decorative arts opened to the public in the 1950s, he and his wife moved to a smaller house he built just across the entry court. "I'm only a visitor at the museum these days," he told a journalist. "But I'm still head gardener at Winterthur." Two years before his death in 1969, Henry Francis du Pont wrote, "My work is in the gardens."

In 2001, with design assistance from landscape architect W. Gary Smith, Winterthur opened Enchanted Woods, an innovative children's garden set in a three-acre wooded glade, once the du Pont daughters' playground. It was a magical way to celebrate the fiftieth anniversary of Winterthur's opening to the public, with special appeal to the next generation of garden visitors.

Sixty acres of historic garden are the green heart of this multifaceted institution. Just as they did when Henry Francis du Pont created the institution, they embrace his former home, now the museum, galleries, and research building. In the half century since his death, the focus has broadened. Natural lands stewardship and environmentally sound horticultural practices are new priorities for its nearly one-thousand-acre historic landscape. In partnership with the Brandywine Conservancy, Winterthur is now protected under a conservation easement. A concerted effort by the grounds staff has increased the size and number of riparian buffers. With reduced mowing, lawn and pasture are morphing back to meadow, and plant diversity is rebounding.

Today, Winterthur's horticulture team honors du Pont's design aesthetic. But the garden is not frozen in time. They seek improved plant varieties just as he did—and would, were he still alive. They plant in his trademark drifts, working to achieve that perfect balance of color, form, and atmosphere. Henry Francis du Pont would be pleased.

LEFT: Artisans fashioned Tulip Tree House from a massive hollow trunk of tulip poplar (*Liriodendron tulipifera*).

OVERLEAF: The Acorn Tearoom, complete with child-sized furnishings for make-believe tea parties, marks the entrance to the Enchanted Woods.

ABOVE: The heritage Sargent cherries (*Prunus sargentii*) hit their stride each April along Garden Lane.

RIGHT: A procession of redbuds underplanted with daffodils lines a curving path on Sycamore Hill overlooking the Quarry Garden.

LEFT: Fragrant spring blossoms of a flowering cherry (*Prunus* 'Hally Jolivette') and magnolias open in the Sundial Garden in early April.

ABOVE: An iron garden sculpture of a blooming lily accents steps within the Sundial Garden.

OVERLEAF, LEFT: Spring and fall hues in the Glade Garden, originally designed as a rustic rock garden by Marian Coffin.

OVERLEAF, RIGHT: Spring peonies fill the garden next to the elegant remains of the original greenhouse complex.

RIGHT: The spring-fed Quarry Garden glows with candelabra primroses (*Primula* species and hybrids) and yellow flag iris (*Iris pseudacorus*) in May.

OVERLEAF: A towering blue Atlas cedar (*Cedrus atlantica* 'Glauca') on the edge of the Pinetum. Henry Francis du Pont once wrote, "I think trees are the greatest asset of the place."

"A Day in Old France"

 The Gardens of Nemours Estate

On Friday, September 16, 1932, residents of Wilmington, Delaware, were abuzz. That Saturday and Sunday, the intriguing and, to many, mysterious Nemours Estate would be open to the public for the first time since Alfred I. du Pont had built it two decades earlier. Anyone with an admission ticket would at last be admitted through the iron gates and see what lay behind those intimidating nine-foot masonry walls topped with jagged if colorful broken bottles. ❃ There was no lack of publicity. The Wilmington *News Journal* promoted the event, printing a long feature story and an aerial photograph of the house and grounds that Friday evening. On N.B.C.'s "Red Network" Radio, listeners tuned in to a special broadcast by Governor Pollard of Virginia, who described a visit to Nemours as "a day in old France."

The owners, Alfred and Jessie Ball du Pont, would be in residence, relatively rare at the time, as they now lived most of the year at their Florida home, Epping Forest.

The du Ponts hoped for a good turnout that weekend. Ticket sales would benefit one of Jessie's favorite charities: historic Stratford Hall, home of three generations of the Lee family in Tidewater Virginia. For his part, Alfred pledged to "match the proceeds dollar for dollar" and donate to local unemployment relief, especially needed during the continuing economic depression. These were just two of Mr. and Mrs. Alfred I. du Pont's many philanthropic activities. He was already beloved in the area—especially by those over 65—for setting up the Delaware Old Age Pension Fund and paying for it out of his own pocket until the state voted it into law. But how many locals, Alfred and Jessie wondered, would pay $1.50 for a chance to see their estate?

They needn't have worried. The weather was fine, and three thousand arrived—mostly by car—over the two days of the event. A "very orderly and nice crowd," noted Jessie in her diary.

What was Nemours like for their visitors? Grand. Even getting from the entrance gate to the house was an experience. It was a planned entry sequence. The driveway was a long corridor flanked with walls of matched trees, the first of many allées they would see on the property. Along the drive, they caught glimpses of the gardens—a bridge here, a colonnade there—tastes of what was to come, like the tiny *amuse-bouches* served before a fine meal.

At the crest of the hill was the mansion. The walk to the house, at a precise ninety-degree angle from the drive, was deliberate and processional. One strolled along the wide, white gravel path among symmetrical evergreens, manicured turf, and marble statuary. A set of antique ironwork gates, ornamented with swirls of gilded oak leaves and the initial "N",

PREVIOUS PAGES: The terraces of the Long Walk shimmer through jets of the Reflecting Pool at Nemours Estate.

ABOVE: Aerial view of Nemours Estate, 1932.

OPPOSITE: The eighteenth-century English gates were once installed at Wimbledon Manor outside London.

OVERLEAF: Green foliage on the allée of red maples (*Acer rubrum*) creates a calm entrance corridor in summer.

provided the transition to the mansion designed by Carrère & Hastings, architects also of the New York Public Library. Its inspiration, it is said, was Marie Antoinette's Petit Trianon palace, built on the grounds of Versailles by her husband, Louis XVI, though it is hardly a copy. It was, however, by far the most palatial of the du Pont residences in Wilmington's surrounds.

Visitors were soon put at ease. The 188th Coast Artillery Band played music both days. Those who climbed the mansion's front steps to the imposing white facade of Indiana limestone columns found comfortable furniture and potted oleanders. That vast shaded portico was, in fact, a comfortable front porch. When they turned around, the view was breathtaking

Down the central axis, the main gardens unrolled. There is a rhythm, which no doubt appealed to Alfred, as an engineer and musician. The Long Walk progressed, with tiered carpets of green lawn or *tapis vert*, punctuated by immense marble planters. The Reflecting Pool served as the family swimming pool. Then the Maze Garden; its imperceptible tilt tricked the eye into looking beyond to the Colonnade, Sunken Garden, and naturalistic lake. The distance was a third of a mile, though it appeared longer. A little circular temple, the "Pavilion d'Amour," terminated the axis. There, a statue of Diana the virgin huntress faced the mansion, a strange choice for a temple of love, but then, Alfred's lifetime of loves and losses was anything but straightforward.

This was a garden in the grand style of the seventeenth-century *jardin français*, of André Le Nôtre and the designers who followed over the next two hundred-plus years, adapting his tightly controlled symmetry to suit the baroque and more modern tastes. It explores the formal possibilities of the French design idiom, translated to Delaware.

As if the main gardens weren't enough, there was much more to the landscape of Nemours. Grapevines shaded a long arbor just past the house, and productive vegetable beds supplied larder and table. The back

PREVIOUS PAGES: *Diana the Huntress* by Jean-Antoine Houdon presides over the Temple of Love surrounded by the burgeoning white azaleas (*Rhododendron* 'Delaware Valley White').

ABOVE AND RIGHT: The mood and colors of the Long Walk change with the season, the weather, and the time of day.

of the mansion looked out to a large rectangular lily pond. The far side had
its parterre—best viewed from the upper floor—plus a cutting garden for
flowers, the rose garden, and a complex of Lord & Burnham greenhouses.
The woodlands were extensive, with hill and dale, streams, and natural
springs; Alfred set up a pumping system for house and garden as well as
a bottling plant for spring water. There was room for everything. The core
estate, surrounded by its infamous wall, was three hundred acres. With
adjoining parcels added over time, it was once well over a thousand.

Alfred du Pont had built and planted Nemours, not for Jessie, but
as a love letter to his previous wife, Alicia Bradford Maddox du Pont. Its

ABOVE: Entrance facade, c. 1910.

LEFT: Patterned mowing in the Four Borders Garden emphasizes the use of perspective in the French-inspired architecture and gardens.

OVERLEAF: An arc of white horse chestnuts (*Aesculus hippocastanum*) and manicured turf shapes the view to the Temple of Love.

style reflected their interest in all things French and their shared French heritage. Its design was well within the abilities of the architect engaged for the job. Thomas Hastings had, after all, trained in Paris and with John Carrère ran the most successful Beaux-Arts architectural firm in America. As Hastings once said, if the house was the main course of a residential property, the garden was "the sauce." Alfred was an active client who collaborated throughout the design and construction of both.

The extended du Pont family did not approve, either of the ostentatious grandeur of the estate or of the marriage—both he and Alicia were divorced. With few exceptions, his relations shunned them. Over time, his cousins also forced him out of the DuPont Company. Yet the always-proud Alfred had christened his new home as a tribute to their collective ancestry.

The gardens at Nemours are at once monumental and personal. The site Alfred chose for the estate was saturated with childhood memories. Out walking in the woods with his father one day, they had come upon a grove of mature tulip poplars. There Papa told young Alfred a secret: he wished he could build a house in the shelter of those trees and retire there, reading books and eating ice cream. Only one of the tulip poplars still survives just below the parterre, an ancient, weathered being. Alfred cherished the trees at Nemours and, with his ample horticultural staff, planted hundreds more: oaks, horse chestnuts, maples, conifers.

Nemours is a theater of memories, some poignant, a few heartbreaking. When he built the estate, Alfred was estranged from all but one of his children, and so the situation remained for decades. He and Alicia tried desperately to have a family of their own. Four babies were born, two boys and two girls, but none survived. In the face of such losses, their marriage was rocky, but the couple shared love for young Alicia—her daughter by her first husband—and Denise whom they adopted from France. There are home movies of the children swimming in the fountain and playing in

LEFT: When Alfred Victor du Pont and Gabriel Massena designed the Sunken Garden, they specified Italian travertine for the structure to complement the Carrara marble sculpture.

ABOVE: A marble birdbath marks the center of the Boxwood Garden parterre.

OVERLEAF: The mixed herbaceous plantings of the Four Borders Garden are replete with iris and peonies in spring.

 131

the Wren's Nest, a playhouse built at the edge of the gardens. Alicia died suddenly in 1920, apparently from a heart attack.

A year later, Alfred married longtime friend Jessie Ball. Twenty years his junior, she encouraged him to reconcile with the children of his first marriage and begin to build relationships with his grandchildren. With "dearest little Jessie," Alfred continued work on the gardens. His son Alfred Victor du Pont, an architect, designed the Sunken Garden, the lake, and the Temple of Love. Ed Ball, Jessie's brother and Alfred's business partner, found the ornate Russian gates, purported to have been Catherine the Great's, and Alfred bought them to balance the English set at the opposite side of the mansion. Jessie loved the gardens.

That September weekend in 1932, between admission tickets and sales from the special shop set up for Stratford Hall literature, they "took in" more than $5,000. Jessie was satisfied. In her diary, she wrote "Dead tired—but happy." She reported one visitor commenting on the garden who had said "there is nothing lovelier in Europe . . . the fitness and poetry of it all." Alfred was pleased. So pleased that within a matter of months, he modified his will adding these instructions for his trustees:

> *It shall be their duty, first, to care for the mansion and grounds and gardens surrounding "Nemours" in order that they be maintained for the pleasure and benefit of the public in their present condition and the grounds improved from time to time . . . and [it] be not permitted to deteriorate, but that it shall consistently become more beautiful and attractive to those who view it as time passes.*

It was a provision that would be in force only three years later. After Alfred's death in 1935, a significant portion of his estimated $40 million estate went to fund a children's hospital on a portion of the Nemours acreage, a hospital Jessie spearheaded and that is clearly visible from the

gardens today. She was also diligent in fulfilling Alfred's wish that Nemours be preserved and open to all. Jessie once said, "A garden should be a source of great joy, as well as a health builder." Her advice: "Work in it daily."

A visit to Nemours is a "day in old France" set in twenty-first-century America. Its gardens are faithful to their history. Yet the challenges are different than in the du Ponts' time. The organization is committed to sustainable cultural stewardship of its gardens, water, and land resources. These projects are where ecological integrity and cultural landscape preservation meet.

Accessibility is also key, adapting historic designed spaces to welcome people of diverse physical abilities, of all ages and backgrounds. Each year more of the graveled paths are converted to surfaces that support rolling devices of all kinds. Financial accessibility is another consideration. With ACCESS Delaware, families using public assistance receive low-cost admission to the estate.

Alfred, Alicia, and Jessie du Pont would be gratified to see the estate's use by a particular audience: the neighboring Nemours Children's Hospital. Estate staff engage in horticultural projects for patients, including the Can-Grow fruit and vegetable garden. A new walking path ushers hospital visitors into the heart of the garden at no charge. For clinical staff and family members, the estate offers temporary reprieve, a respite especially apparent during the Covid-19 crisis.

For any visitor on any day, Nemours is indeed "a health builder," and "a source of great joy." Walking the property, with its calm symmetry, beautiful vistas, and shady nooks, is a healing experience, an encounter with cultivated nature at its most benign.

The gardens of Nemours Estate are an important healing resource for the adjacent Nemours Children's Hospital, Delaware.

PREVIOUS PAGES, LEFT: A series of interconnected ponds and waterways forms a reflective necklace between the Sunken Garden and the Temple of Love.

PREVIOUS PAGES, ABOVE RIGHT: Carmine azaleas contrast with the green veil of spring.

PREVIOUS PAGES, BELOW RIGHT: Distinctive blooms of red horse chestnuts (*Aesculus* x *carnea*) brighten the landscape in May.

LEFT: The lake mirrors the Humpback Bridge and weeping Higan cherries (*Prunus* x *subhirtella* 'Pendula').

OVERLEAF: Two cast-iron elk by French sculptor Prosper Lecourtier punctuate the Long Walk.

139

ABOVE: *Achievement* by sculptor Henri Crenier strides forward at the center of the Maze Garden and is the major focal point of the Long Walk.

RIGHT: The Maze Garden is ablaze with salvias in summer.

OVERLEAF: Canna Tropicanna® ignites the summer planting at the base of the Tendresse Wall.

ABOVE: The Horseshoe Fountain faces the entry court to the house across the main drive. Beyond is the picturesque Water Tower.

RIGHT: From the main drive gravel paths along the *tapis vert* lead through the English gates to the entrance steps and front portico.

ABOVE: The Italian limestone Colonnade displays bas-relief portraits of Pierre Samuel du Pont de Nemours and Éleuthère Irénée du Pont.

LEFT: Cannas add stature to the Golden Privet in the Maze Garden in late summer.

OVERLEAF, ABOVE LEFT: Fall foliage burnishes the landscape on a quiet autumn afternoon.

OVERLEAF, BELOW LEFT: A cherished tulip poplar (*Liriodendron tulipifera*) once admired by Alfred I. du Pont's father anchors the Four Borders Garden.

OVERLEAF, RIGHT: A simple gate opens onto a garden of Asian influences.

Dogwoods and azaleas
bloom near the canopy of
a specimen sycamore
(*Platanus occidentalis*).

PLANTS OF THE PIEDMONT

 *Mt. Cuba Center*

ON MARCH 2, 1965, LAMMOT DU PONT COPELAND WROTE A letter to Seth Kelsey, a Massachusetts nurseryman and former classmate from Harvard. It was an invitation to come to Mt. Cuba for a job interview. The position: managing the gardens, grounds, and a staff of fourteen at Copeland's Delaware estate, Mt. Cuba. In the letter, Copeland first voiced an intention to turn his 280-acre property into a public garden. It would be "privately endowed," he mused, and "something considerably less formal than either Longwood Gardens or Winterthur." This was not his first land-centered philanthropy. ❋ Three years earlier, he and Henry Belin du Pont III had created the Red Clay Reservation. Its purpose was to preserve open space in the Red Clay Creek corridor, which runs from Unionville, Pennsylvania, through Mt. Cuba to the Christina River.

They were at the leading edge of an energized environmental movement, well before the inaugural 1970 Earth Day celebration. Opening Mt. Cuba to the public would go a step further, transforming his family home, gardens, and grounds into a venue for visitors and students of all ages.

Copeland and his wife had been shaping the grounds of Mt. Cuba for more than three decades. When they purchased the land in the 1930s, they had been drawn to its rolling topography. Pamela Copeland, who had grown up in Litchfield, Connecticut, remembered, "Being a New Englander, I felt I must have a hill."

Their architects, the husband-and-wife team Samuel Eldon Homsey and Victorine du Pont Homsey, made splendid use of that hill. They sited the colonial revival residence at the crest, taking in the widest view. Visitors today, standing on the terrace outside the brick center hall, are flanked by a magnificent pair of willow oaks and surrounded by symmetrical beds filled with combinations of perennials native to the region. The vista is idyllic: gently undulating lawns descending the slope, embraced by white pines and native hollies, to meadows and woodlands below.

It bears little resemblance to what the Copelands first saw. They looked out on cornfields, interspersed with a few stands of trees, open down to Barley Mill Road. Pamela Copeland described the tract as "barren." The couple was undaunted. She was already a gardening enthusiast, an interest shared by Lammot, who would rise to become chairman of the DuPont Company.

For planning and planting, they engaged Thomas Sears, an established Philadelphia landscape architect. He worked on the initial grading and installed screening belts of white pine and hemlock, as well as laying out a lilac walk, cutting and vegetable gardens, a small orchard, and a modest greenhouse. With the help of a local nurseryman, the Copelands installed a rock garden.

PREVIOUS PAGES: Mt. Cuba Center's woodland trails invite visitors to explore its naturalistic gardens.

RIGHT: Planters of Berry Timeless hybrid alumroot (*Heuchera* 'Berry Timeless') bracket the view from the terrace across the rolling Piedmont hills. The large ram's head urns were purchased by the Copelands in the late 1940s.

ABOVE: Aerial view of Mt. Cuba, late 1940s.

RIGHT: The pastoral heritage of the region is echoed in Mt. Cuba's landscape.

OVERLEAF: The Round Garden glows with a border of tulips and Emerald Blue moss phlox (*Phlox subulata* 'Emerald Blue') in spring.

In 1949 they invited Marian Coffin to create formal gardens near the house. She had come highly recommended. Henry Francis du Pont–Lammot's cousin–lauded her as "the very best and most imaginative landscape architect." For the Copelands, she designed a series of elegant outdoor rooms, intentional architected spaces with terraced gardens, long borders, brick walks, seating walls, and elegant statuary. A pool in the shape of a Maltese cross was ornamental but deep enough for swimming. Her detailed planting plan, unified by "subtle color modulations and contrasts," was her signature mix of annuals, perennials, shrubs, and trees–both native and non-native species.

It was Coffin who introduced the Copelands to using sweeps of a single type of plant in color gradation. At Mt. Cuba, she employed the device with an extensive border of azaleas ranging from yellow through orange, red, and bronze. As Coffin wrote in her book *Trees and Shrubs for Landscape Effects*, "The combinations and variations on these themes are endless." The Copelands and their gardening staff continued to follow her concept as they extended the gardens on their own.

It was not until the early 1960s, after the Copelands had purchased adjoining acreage with a meadow and large woodlot, that they adopted the naturalistic style for which Mt. Cuba is now justifiably famous. The seventeen-plus acre West Slope, next to the entry drive and front courtyard, was mostly devoid of plantings, but they envisioned a wild garden in contrast to the formality near the house. The Copelands began to develop it with the idea of opening the property to the public as a "botanical park."

But not just any botanical park. They wanted their beloved home to be distinct from other gardens in the northeast including, if not especially, the other du Pont gardens in the neighborhood. In 1965, with the help of their gardening staff, their architects, and Seth Kelsey, who had accepted Copeland's offer, they set to work on the West Slope.

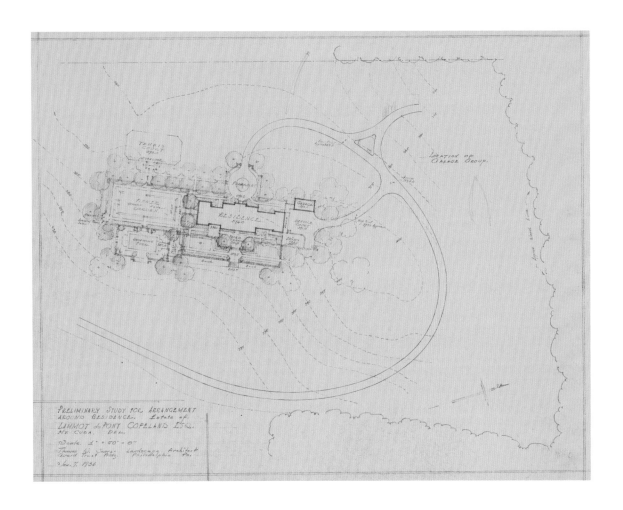

ABOVE: An early Thomas Sears site and garden plan for Mt. Cuba, 1936.

RIGHT: In 2015 the herbaceous borders in the South Garden were redesigned to showcase native plants in a formal garden setting.

Kelsey documented the approach in a memorandum to the Copelands: "Proposed Horticulture Program at Mt. Cuba," dated June 9, 1965. It was to be a picturesque, flowering woodland garden, encouraging education and access to nature. In it, he wrote "at least one limited area might be devoted exclusively to the flora of the Piedmont area so that people may see the kinds of plants that they are likely to find growing here naturally or that grew here before man so largely destroyed them." This is the first hint of what would become Mt. Cuba's future focus on native plants.

The West Slope paths curved along the contour lines, meandering in a naturalistic style that echoed a Japanese stroll garden. "The charm of a trail is its ups and downs to me," Pamela Copeland once explained. Along the Woods Path, they edited and added trees, built ponds and brooks with a recirculating water system, and installed massive wild garden plantings. They crafted the experience. The garden would unfold with transitions and surprises, like an Asian scroll painting.

The Copelands were active participants in the process. Pamela, more often at home, took charge of day-to-day decisions and did her share of planting and weeding. Rare disagreements arose, as when she came upon a quarry road construction project Lammot had initiated before he left on a trip. Picking up her pen, she wrote her spouse with pointed observations. "I had expected a foot path or trail," she explained. "Frankly I don't see the objection to walking single-file. I think one is apt to be more observant than when one walks side by side. And it leaves less of a scar in the woodland." Characteristic of the Copelands' harmonious relationship, a compromise solution was reached.

Wildflowers had been a particular interest of Pamela Copeland since childhood. In the woodland garden, Mt. Cuba's gardeners planted masses of foamflower (*Tiarella cordifolia*), bleeding heart (*Dicentra eximia*), and hepatica in sweeps of which Marian Coffin would have approved. Once

LEFT: Japanese primrose (*Primula japonica*), a non-native plant favored by the Copelands, mingles with Piedmont natives including woodland phlox (*Phlox divaricata*) and golden ragwort (*Packera aurea*).

OVERLEAF, LEFT: Foamflower (*Tiarella cordifolia*) demonstrates its beauty as a reliable native ground cover for shade.

OVERLEAF, RIGHT: Spring sunlight picks out the white bracts on a mature flowering dogwood (*Cornus florida*) in the Meadow on the West Slope.

established, the plantings would naturalize into spreading colonies of their own. Ground covers filled gaps, such as native pachysandra (*P. procumbens*), yellowroot (*Xanthorhiza simplicissima*), and variegated goutweed (*Lamium galeobdolon* 'Variegatum'), a Eurasian member of the mint family.

In the early decades of development, native and introduced species continued to be commingled at Mt. Cuba. Native dogwood (*Cornus florida*) and silverbell (*Halesia montana*) arrived, along with magnolias and flowering cherries that traced their origins to Asia. Rhododendron and azalea plantings—originally conceived as trial gardens for the Rhododendron Society—included many Asian hybrids alongside their North American kin. Showy Japanese primroses (*Primula japonica*), one of Lammot Copeland's favorites, would bloom each May, intermingling with native pitcher plants and marsh marigolds (*Caltha palustris*) in the wet margins around the ponds.

As the gardens evolved, the Mt. Cuba arborists pruned lower branches on the mature trees. Lifting the canopy admitted more light to the understory. A side benefit was the "cathedral effect." With their substantial girth, the tall, straight trunks of the tulip poplars (*Liriodendron tulipifera*), oaks, and other tree species convey the impression of columns in a great hall or cathedral. The horticultural staff took advantage of the new light conditions, amending and expanding the understory's plantings.

Moving down the West Slope from the drive and entry courtyard, today's visitor meanders along shaded paths. They seem to melt into nature untouched: pristine forest, marsh, and meadow. It is skillful sleight of hand and entirely man-made. The occasional sign or structure—a bridge, a bench, the gazebo that overlooks a pond—reveals the secret.

Through reading, garden visits, Longwood courses, and decades of hands-on experience, Pamela Copeland had gained considerable expertise in horticulture. She then turned her attention to becoming an informed conservationist, particularly of Delaware's wildflowers. In 1982 the Copelands

The combined effect of sun and tall tulip trees (*Liriodendron tulipifera*) in the naturalistic Woods Path gardens is awe-inspiring.

168

invited Dr. Richard Lighty, a plant geneticist and then director of the Longwood Graduate Program at the University of Delaware, to consult with them on opening Mt. Cuba to the public. It was Lighty, Pamela Copeland remembered, who "suggested enlarging the scope of [our] concerns from native Delaware flora exclusively to that of the whole Piedmont region."

After Lammot Copeland's death in 1983, Dr. Lighty became the first director of the newly christened Mt. Cuba Center for the Study of Piedmont Flora. Pamela Copeland continued to work closely with him and his successor: setting up a foundation, developing the gardens, and planning for visitor access and facilities. The property remained her private estate, open for occasional prearranged visits, until her death in 2001. Mt. Cuba's next incarnation, as a public garden and research center, then began in earnest. It has accelerated since.

Many gardeners know Mt. Cuba for its large-scale native plant trials and research reports. Its experts evaluate Piedmont genera, most recently "Hydrangea for the Mid-Atlantic Region." They propagated, planted, and monitored twenty-nine species and cultivars of native hydrangea. Their research answers questions critical to ecological gardening: Which do pollinators prefer? Which perform best for home gardeners, and in which growing conditions? Their readable summary reports are widely publicized and available free of charge on the Mt. Cuba website.

As the Copelands had envisioned, Mt. Cuba Center teaches fluency in wild plants of the Piedmont. Its education program will soon celebrate its twentieth birthday. Students come for courses on everything from native plant identification and horticultural techniques to botanical painting and yoga. Landscape professionals and dedicated backyard gardeners can complete a comprehensive program to earn a certificate in ecological gardening.

Lammot and Pamela Copeland would still recognize their gardens. Their original selections are honored as heritage plantings. Japanese

LEFT: Rhododendron (*Rhododendron* spp.) and native mountain laurel (*Kalmia latifolia*) plantings share the stage with woodland wildflowers on the West Slope Path.

OVERLEAF, LEFT: Mt. Cuba's Trial Garden evaluates native plants and their related cultivars for horticultural and ecological value.

OVERLEAF, ABOVE RIGHT: *Longwood Purple* American wisteria (*Wisteria frutescens* 'Longwood Purple') winds around the Trial Garden fence.

OVERLEAF, BELOW RIGHT: In 2022 a trial was underway for goldenrod (*Solidago* spp.) and related species.

flowering cherries still grace the entry drive. The formal garden is now planted with Mid-Atlantic shrubs and perennials in an English perennial garden aesthetic, though a few of Marian Coffin's sweeps of Asian azaleas are still carefully tended. They would still find tulips filling the bracketing beds of the swimming pool in spring, a bedding scheme that changes with the season. But the circular borders beyond are filled with native species that support the local pollinator population and ecosystem: drifts of black-eyed Susans (*Rudbeckia* spp.), coneflowers (*Echinacea* spp.), *Amsonia*, *Phlox*, grasses and more—a pleasing mix, but different than in their time. Guests now enter through a new Woodland Glade, designed by the landscape architecture firm Nelson Byrd Woltz. New sustainable greenhouse and nursery facilities will soon support more research, propagation, and production of native plants.

Mt. Cuba is renowned in spring, as North America's woodland ephemerals peak. The songs of migratory birds enliven the grounds. It is a glorious time to see Mt. Cuba, but as the year unfolds, it is equally glorious. Orange Turk's-cap lilies (*Lilium superbum*) stand tall atop eight-foot stems in July, attracting hummingbirds and visitors. The meadow is energized in summer and fully alive by autumn, abuzz with pollinators and a magnet for butterflies. Fall color ignites the tree canopy and the forest edge. In any season, native flora resonates with the scenery, tied to place. Its intimacy appeals to gardeners, artists, photographers, and anyone in need of a dose of nature.

In 2018 the Copelands' two notable conservation efforts, Mt. Cuba Center and the Red Clay Reservation merged. Mt. Cuba now stewards more than one thousand acres: the original estate plus some 800 acres of northern Delaware's natural land, much of it former farmland. Several miles of trails traverse grasslands, forest, and forest edge habitats, a complement to the curated display gardens. To visit Mt. Cuba is to dive into nature, to revisit our place on the planet.

RIGHT: In autumn, a screen of hair-awn muhly grass (*Muhlenbergia capillaris*) and an arch of Winter King green hawthorn (*Crataegus viridis* 'Winter King') offer glimpses of the Round Garden.

OVERLEAF: The hand-forged entry gates, created by local artisans Greg Leavitt and his daughter Camille, incorporate motifs of native plants.

ABOVE: Eagle sculptures on the forecourt's brick pillars face the pink blooms of one of the Copelands' weeping Higan cherries (*Prunus* x *subhirtella* 'Pendula').

LEFT: The Scree Garden, completed in 2008, features native plants such as Little Lanterns wild columbine (*Aquilegia canadensis* 'Little Lanterns'), moss phlox (*Phlox subulata*), and large fothergilla (*Fothergilla major*).

LEFT: The contemporary planting design for the South Garden picks up the color of the original brick walls and walks.

OVERLEAF, LEFT: Aromatic aster (*Symphyotrichum oblongifolium*) fills one section of the Lower Oak Allée in autumn.

OVERLEAF, RIGHT: Jeana garden phlox (*Phlox paniculata* 'Jeana'), Rocky Top Tennessee purple coneflower (*Echinacea tennesseensis* 'Rocky Top'), and black-eyed Susan (*Rudbeckia fulgida* var. *fulgida*) are standouts in this sunny Round Garden border.

ABOVE: A stand of lesser yellow lady's slipper orchids (*Cypripedium parviflorum* var. *parviflorum*) makes a statement in mid-May.

RIGHT: Appalachian Red redbud (*Cercis canadensis* 'Appalachian Red') and flowering dogwood complement yellow celandine poppies (*Stylophorum diphyllum*) and blue Jacob's ladder (*Polemonium reptans*) on the way to the Woods Path.

OVERLEAF, LEFT: A flame azalea (*Rhododendron calendulaceum*) opens with bright orange blooms near the pond in late spring.

OVERLEAF, RIGHT: Pamela Copeland used "mailboxes" to leave notes about her observations for the gardeners; today visitors can find activities for all ages inside them.

ABOVE: Both wild hydrangea (*Hydrangea arborescens*) and goldenrod (*Solidago* spp.) offer attractive flowers and excellent support for pollinators.

RIGHT: A foggy morning mist lends an extra luster to the pond's surface.

OVERLEAF: The Copelands placed the gazebo by the pond as a place to contemplate, congregate, and take in the view.

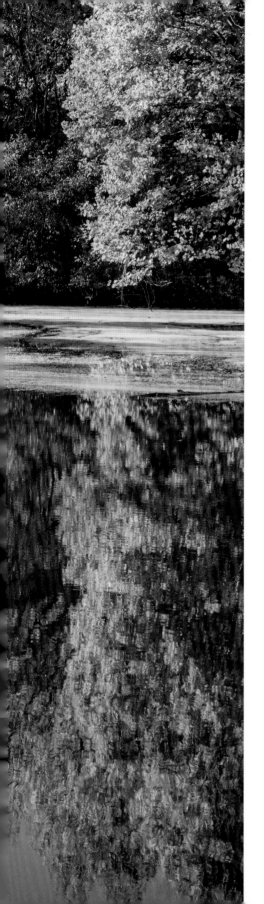

LEFT: In Mt. Cuba's thousand-acre natural lands, a still pond captures a cloudless sky and the changing leaf colors of autumn.

ABOVE: American white waterlilies (*Nymphaea odorata*) create a flotilla of lily pads and blooms on the surface of one of the ponds.

OVERLEAF, LEFT: The remnants of a historic stone farmhouse lend character to the landscape.

OVERLEAF, RIGHT: Along the West Slope Path, arborists artfully sculpted the stump of a removed tree, incorporating it into the garden's design.

Epic Landscapes

 *Longwood Gardens*

ALL GARDENS ARE THEATER, BUT SOME GARDENS ARE MORE theatrical than others. In the case of Longwood Gardens, even its origin story is dramatic. For Pierre S. du Pont, it was a rescue mission for a group of extraordinary trees. ✳ In July 1906, the thirty-six-year-old du Pont confessed to an attack of temporary insanity. He had purchased not just real estate, but a farm. And not just any farm, but the "old Peirce place," an eighteenth-century farmstead-turned-arboretum near Kennett Square, Pennsylvania. Busy as an executive with the DuPont Company, which he and his cousins had purchased four years earlier, he had acquired the 202-acre property "to save the collection of old trees." The trees, he explained, "had been accumulated by the Peirce family over a period of more than one hundred years, many of them of extraordinary growth and arresting appearance." They had been destined for the lumber mill.

His farm, he admitted, was a "a very pretty place." The terrain was varied, with field, forest, and lakes. The old brick farmhouse, set amid its mature woods, could be his weekend retreat, "a place where I can entertain my friends." He christened his new home "Longwood," a local place-name used by several properties including the nearby Longwood Meeting House built by abolitionist Quakers before the Civil War. The MIT-trained du Pont, an industrialist experienced in engineering, finance, and management, then turned some of his prodigious spare energy to designing gardens.

A year later, he had laid out a six-hundred-foot flower border south and west of the historic Peirce trees. It was a conservative start. Two linear beds flanked a long gravel path. Plantings were blocks of old-fashioned flowers, outlined with box borders. At the height of spring, red poppies and blue irises made their vivid statement. He crowned his design with a circular pool, twenty feet in diameter. A single ribbon of water rose from its center. To supply the jet, water was pumped via hydraulic ram from Longwood's Large Lake to a tank in the attic of the house; from there, gravity took over. It was du Pont's first fountain in his first garden. It was only the beginning.

In his early years at Longwood, he added garden rooms in his usual disciplined and methodical fashion. It was as if he were creating a quilt, pieced in the tidy geometry of French and Italian traditions. A sunken garden contributed variety with a terrace, wide steps, and a square reflecting pool. The Rose Garden had pyramidal conifers and cedar arbors for structure, complementing the blooms of its namesake plants. For an exploration of green, the Sundial Garden offered parterres of turf grass outlined in dwarf boxwood.

He modernized and expanded the house. He planted more trees. Soon he began to entertain, his guests reinforcing his gardening ambitions with their attention, their praise. His annual garden party became *the* summer event for Wilmington society.

PREVIOUS PAGES: The sunken marble floor of the Exhibition Hall in the Main Conservatory can be flooded with water to shimmer beneath horticultural treasures.

ABOVE: A mix of deciduous trees and conifers at Peirce's Park, 1913.

OPPOSITE: The largest of Longwood's Atlas cedars (*Cedrus atlantica*) arrived in 1930 as seven-foot specimens for planting on the Conifer Knoll behind the Main Fountain Garden.

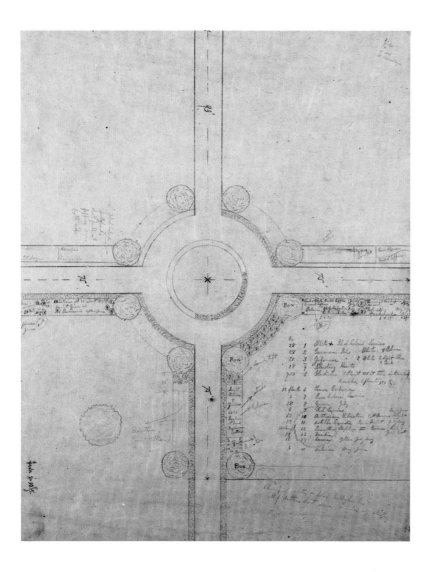

ABOVE: Pierre S. du Pont's drawing of the Flower Garden Walk, 1907.

RIGHT: Spires of foxglove (*Digitalis* Illumination Flame™ and *Digitalis purpurea* 'Dalmatian Peach') mimic the single jet of the Round Fountain in mid-spring.

Always striving for spectacle at Longwood, du Pont was open to inspiration. Since childhood, he had been taken with gardening under glass, appreciating the grand architecture and fountain technology at successive world's fairs across the country including the 1876 Centennial Exposition in Philadelphia, the World's Columbian in Chicago in 1893, and the St. Louis celebration of the Louisiana Purchase in 1904. It was new garden technology, hydraulics and electricity, for a new century. He could tap into these ideas for his own garden plans.

And then there was European travel. A black-and-white photograph dated February 1913 shows a smiling Pierre clad in a long coat and jaunty driving cap on the stage of the *teatro di verzura*, the outdoor theater at the seventeenth-century Villa Gori in Siena. Family members pose on either elbow: on the left, his younger sister, Margaretta du Pont Carpenter, and leaning in on his right, his cousin, diminutive Alice Belin, with whom he shared many interests, particularly their French heritage. They would marry in October 1915. Meanwhile, when he returned to America that winter of 1913, du Pont set to work on his own Open Air Theatre, borrowing liberally from Siena.

On Thursday, June 25, 1914, *The Early Evening* of Wilmington reported on Longwood's garden party, held in Kennett Square the previous evening. More than three hundred guests–family, friends, and business associates–gathered at the Open Air Theatre for its premier performance. The journalist compared it to entertainments at an eighteenth-century fête at the Palace of Versailles. "Just at dark electric lights were turned on simultaneously illuminating the stage in front and sides, and a spotlight discovered four couples descending from the terrace above the stage to the classic strains of Beethoven's music." It was a program of costumed dances–minuet, Italian folk dance, and gavotte. The finale was grand, "a frolic by the harlequins who, much to the surprise of the guests, danced

ABOVE: Main Fountain Garden, 1928.

OPPOSITE: Twelve pedestal basin fountains flank the Italian Water Garden in the shade of little-leaf lindens (*Tilia cordata*).

OVERLEAF, ABOVE LEFT: Open Air Theatre, 1928.

OVERLEAF, BELOW LEFT: Open Air Theatre with dancers, 1915.

OVERLEAF, RIGHT: Audiences of up to 1,500 continue to enjoy performances and fountain displays in the Open Air Theatre.

among them, throwing confetti and garden roses, then winding their way out in a path of light, finally disappearing amid the trees."

Pierre du Pont knew how to deliver a crowd-pleaser. But he was not finished with the Theatre, over the years adding a perimeter arcade of American Pillar roses, spacious below-ground dressing rooms, and illuminated fountains. A ten-foot-high water curtain screened and revealed the performers. More than seven hundred water jets delivered a menu of special effects, including bursts of compressed air that shot water fifty feet skyward. With seating capacity of fifteen hundred, the Theatre has been a venue for countless artists including du Pont's friend John Philip Sousa and his band, the Philadelphia Orchestra under the baton of Eugene Ormandy, and Wynton Marsalis's Jazz at Lincoln Center. Gilbert and Sullivan operettas were a du Pont favorite, and the Savoy Company of Philadelphia obliged, a tradition that began in 1916 and continues to the present.

Du Pont once again expanded the Peirce house, welcoming his bride into a residence doubled in size and graced by his first conservatory: an arched atrium of glass joining the old wing to the new. Alice and Pierre enjoyed their home. A Bryn Mawr graduate, she shared his zeal for gardening. Like Pierre, she was an indefatigable entertainer. Longwood Gardens became a magnet for garden enthusiasts, school groups, and civic groups, as well as family and friends. She was a capable, gracious host, welcoming guests to Longwood events with aplomb, even when business demands prevented Pierre's participation. She inspired and encouraged his steady application of time and resources to new Longwood projects.

Some were suggested by their continued travels. From 1925 to 1927, he created the Italian Water Garden after the plan of the Villa Gamberaia, visited on their tour of Tuscany. It is an elaborate homage to its celebrated water parterres. His design, with its six hundred jets and a water staircase, is more elaborate and exuberant than the original.

The Peirce-du Pont House, seen through a scrim of magnolia blossoms.

ABOVE: Villa Gamberaia, near Florence, Italy, c. 1920.

RIGHT: A taste of Tuscany in Kennett Square, the Italian Water Garden is a dynamic interplay of moving water and sunlight.

A garden is the mirror of its creator, and Longwood reflects Pierre du Pont's personality. He thrived on technical challenges, but more than that, he enjoyed sharing the results, revealing the latest accomplishment at his annual garden party. The Main Conservatory complex, unveiled in 1921, would provide year-round space for breathtaking displays. Tended by members of the Horticultural Department led by du Pont's long-tenured English head gardener William Mulliss, there were acacias dripping with golden blooms, camellias, amaryllis, quantities of chrysanthemums, a Christmas tree in December. Its Exhibition Hall had a vast marble floor that could be flooded with a thin mirroring surface of water or drained for flower shows, banquets, concerts, and charity events in any weather.

The Conservatory seemed to never stop growing, nor did the number of people who came to see it. There was a house dedicated to roses, another to orchids—Alice du Pont was an avid collector and longtime board member of the American Orchid Society—and production houses for fruits and vegetables. An amateur musician, du Pont built the Music Room behind the Exhibition Hall, and, in 1930, installed a 10,010-pipe Aeolian organ in the newly constructed Ballroom.. The du Ponts delighted in hosting world-class musicians to play for Longwood concerts.

Outside the Conservatory, Pierre du Pont built the culmination of his hydraulic endeavors: the huge Main Fountain Garden, with two canals and a classically inspired loggia topped by even bigger fountains. A purpose-built reservoir and pumping station recirculated thousands of gallons a minute to the countless basins and masses of jets. The special effects were breathtaking by day; by night, it was awe-inspiring, lit by custom-made high-intensity glass bulbs with filters in five colors. A *Philadelphia Inquirer* article described the after-dusk fountain shows as "a fairyland of light-come-alive." It was a fantasy constructed between 1929 and 1931, more than two decades before Walt Disney broke ground for Disneyland. Fountain

ABOVE: Waterlilies, including the giant pads of *Victoria amazonica*, fill the Waterlily Display.

OPPOSITE: Acacia Passage is a memorable experience in the Conservatory in late winter, a tunnel of cinnamon wattle (*Acacia leprosa*) with a parade of daffodil planters and round baskets of yellow *Guzmania* 'Depladia' Diana.

OVERLEAF: An evening performance at the Main Fountain Garden is a magical, magnificent kingdom of sound, light, and hydraulics.

shows are a perennial favorite, running daily in season, weather permitting. Now, after an exhaustive renovation and preservation from 2014 to 2017, computer-controlled with robotics, LED lighting, a sound system, and fireworks on special occasions, the illuminated spectacles continue to dazzle visitors on summer and autumn evenings.

To complement the fountain terrace, du Pont commissioned a Longwood-scale backdrop: a fifty-foot waterfall and an instant landscape. Several hundred full-grown trees and shrubs arrived to transform what had been a sloping cornfield. A carillon still chimes today from the stone bell tower, the highest point of the composition.

The du Ponts were generous in welcoming visitors, who came in large numbers once the Conservatory opened in 1921. Acquiring contiguous parcels during his lifetime, Pierre du Pont had expanded Longwood to nearly one thousand acres, including the neighboring Merrick and Webb farms, which he used for orchards, crop production, and livestock. He also had the acumen to prepare the legal and financial instruments necessary to continue Longwood's trajectory as a non-profit institution. Millions of guests have visited Longwood Gardens since then. And, as du Pont had envisioned, Longwood's programs have educated generations of horticulturists and public garden managers.

In 1925 Claude Monet had shown the du Ponts his waterlilies at Giverny. Pierre du Pont never got around to a waterlily planting at Longwood. It wasn't until a few years after his death in 1954 that waterlilies first bloomed in the ponds of the water terrace outside the Conservatory. In his ambitious spirit, management and staff reimagined gardens, mounted new exhibitions, and improved visitor facilities.

Pierre S. du Pont, whether running the DuPont Company, General Motors, or Longwood, never turned away from a challenge. In 2014 Longwood opened its 86-acre Meadow Garden. It had been no mean feat.

From April to October, the waterfall cascades from Oak and Conifer Knoll to the basin at the foot of Chimes Tower.

The two decade-plus effort had involved the Pennsylvania Department of Transportation relocating a substantial stretch of Route 52, a two-lane highway. There had been precedent. Annoyed with the poor-quality toll road between Wilmington and Longwood, du Pont had acquired the hundred-year-old Kennett Pike from its shareholders in 1916. He rebuilt the roadbed, eliminated the tolls, banned billboards, then gave the respective portions to the states of Delaware and Pennsylvania. It is now a designated part of the Brandywine Valley Scenic Byway.

The lush Meadow at Longwood Gardens with its mowed trails and boardwalk, now brings walkers in close communion with the landscape. It echoes its origins. The Lenni-Lenape had known it as mixed woodland and savanna. The Webb family had farmed it, as had du Pont in later years. The stone farmhouse built by the Webbs is now the Meadow's focal point, repurposed as a gallery. The Meadow Garden is a small, accessible part of the institution's land stewardship program, with seven hundred acres of open space under management.

Many of Longwood's signature attractions—the Topiary Garden and Hillside Garden, A Longwood Christmas, "Nature's Castles" tree houses, the Eye of Water, and more—were realized under one of the four chief executives who have led the organization since the 1950s. During the past seventy years, well-known landscape architects have renewed old garden spaces and created new ones. Thomas Church, Roberto Burle Marx, Isabelle Greene, and W. Gary Smith are just a few of the designers who have had a hand in its current guise. The glasshouse complex continues to grow, with seventeen acres of reimagined gardens and the West Conservatory due for completion in 2024. There are new plant collections, research initiatives, and infrastructure projects addressing contemporary concerns, such as habitat loss and the climate crisis. Longwood Gardens is truly a world apart. A world of beauty. A better world.

RIGHT: Trails through the Meadow Garden lead through wetlands, ponds, open fields, and the forest edge. Exhibits in the historic Webb Farmhouse explore the landscape through the seasons and the stories of the people who have inhabited and influenced the land since the Lenni-Lenape.

OVERLEAF, LEFT: Japanese wisteria (*Wisteria floribunda*) are shaped into tiered tree forms in the Wisteria Garden, designed by landscape architect Thomas Church in 1976.

OVERLEAF, RIGHT: Ivory fritillaries and crown imperials (*Fritillaria persica* 'Ivory Bells' and *F. imperialis* 'Aurora') float over a sea of daffodils.

RIGHT: More than 200,000 tulips
are part of the Spring Blooms display
at Longwood Gardens each year.

OVERLEAF: Poet's narcissus
(*N. poeticus*), purple ornamental
onions (*Allium hollandicum* 'Purple
Sensation'), and yellow columbine
(*Aquilegia* 'Swan Yellow') are
front and center in this swath of
spring glory.

ABOVE: The 1929 stone Chimes Tower is a backdrop to the defined spaces of the Idea Garden.

LEFT: An exuberant mixed border is the foreground for the precise shapes of mature sheared yews (*Taxus baccata*) in the Topiary Garden.

225

RIGHT: Pierre S. du Pont planted this Japanese flowering dogwood (*Cornus kousa*), now a Pennsylvania Champion Tree, near the Open Air Theatre.

OVERLEAF, LEFT: The Florentine firm A. Olivotti & Co. provided the Renaissance-inspired carved limestone features of the Main Fountain Garden in the 1930s.

OVERLEAF, RIGHT: Iconic 'American Pillar' rambling roses arch over the circular Rose Arbor, creating a striking space for guests to enjoy.

ABOVE: In late summer, this corner of Flower Garden Walk is awash with the greenish-yellows of angel's-trumpet (*Brugmansia* 'Cypress Gardens') and flowering tobacco (*Nicotiana* 'Lime Green').

LEFT: This Chinese scholar tree (*Styphnolobium japonicum*), purchased from Moon Nursery near Philadelphia in 1928, is now among the largest of this species in the region.

ABOVE: The Birdhouse, an Adirondack-style tree house, offers a 360-degree view of the forest canopy morning, afternoon, or evening.

RIGHT: A rock-edged creek is a constructed landscape, channeling the water flow between the reservoir and the Pear-Shaped Basin.

OVERLEAF: The dusty pink flowers of Joe-Pye-weed (*Eutrochium fistulosum*) tower above warm season grasses and forbs in the Meadow Garden late in the growing season.

ACKNOWLEDGMENTS

This book would not have been initiated or completed without the insight and help of Rodman Ward Jr. He invited me to do the project and brought the five independent gardens together. Unfortunately, he passed away in March 2023 before he could see this book completed. Rod was a visionary. His genius was the ability to see what should be done and to get it done and have everyone involved appreciate the opportunity to participate. Much that he touched will last because of such generosity of spirit.

A long list of people from these great gardens contributed mightily to the development of this book:

From Longwood Gardens: Paul B. Redman, President and CEO, was always gracious and available to guide me and coordinate with the other gardens; Marnie Conley, Chief Experience and Brand Officer, managed the Longwood effort; Jackie Miller, Tour Guide Supervisor, was my guide on substantially all my visits to Longwood, amazing me with her knowledge of the history and horticulture of the gardens and the best ways to experience them; Marianne McNeice also knowledgeably guided me. Colvin Randall, P. S. du Pont Fellow, David Sleasman, Director, Library and Information Services, Maureen McCadden, prior Digital Resource Manager, and Kristina Aguilar, Associate Director, Plant Information and Mapping, made valuable contributions to the text.

From Mt. Cuba Center: Jeff Downing, Executive Director, regularly took me around and shared his vision for the historic garden (and its mission) and the immense natural lands. Sometimes I felt we were on horseback in his Jeep as we traversed difficult terrain. These were good times that will not be forgotten. Amy Highland, Director of Collections and Conservation Lead, was an important resource.

From Winterthur: Chris Strand guided me through this great garden and shared its history while he was Director of Gardens & Estate; when he became CEO, he always had a working lunch with me on my visits. I count him as a friend. Linda Eirhart, Nicole Schmid, Carol Long, and Collin Hadsell, knowledgeable plantspeople all, showed me the seasonal wonders from visit to visit. Jeff Groff, Estate Historian, shared his deep knowledge of the property.

From Nemours: Jean Hershner, Executive Director, set up the arrangements and made sure that my visits were productive. Kenneth Darsney, Horticultural Supervisor, took me around and shared his vision with me; Ray Murphy, a gardener and man of many talents, was my regular guide and served brilliantly for Marta and me as the Nemours historian.

From Hagley: Jill Mackenzie, Executive Director, was very supportive and made things easy for me when there were severe challenges from nature. Paul Orpello, Director of Gardens and Horticulture, guided me and opened up the Crowninshield Garden and passed along his excitement and hopes for its restoration. Marsha Mills, Foundation Archivist, provided valuable insights. Marketing Manager Laura Jury facilitated many of my days there.

With utmost appreciation to my editor Elizabeth White, whose judgment is superb and who has artfully guided me through numerous books; to Marta McDowell, who has written the lucid text and captions, making the history come alive and thus given the photographs their proper frame; and to Susi Oberhelman, whose elegant design weaves the text and images together.

With great gratitude to John Maggiotto, a master printer, photographer, and teacher, who has worked with me on all my books and taught me much.

With love and affection to my wife, Kitty Hawks, fondly known as Hawkeye, who has refined my taste over our many years together and helped me grow into my ambitions.

LARRY LEDERMAN

All photographs are by Larry Lederman except as noted below
Carrère & Hastings Collection, American Academy of Arts & Letters: 127
Hagley Museum and Library: 29, 49, 52, 57, 58, 62, 64, 67, 117, 158, 199, 203, 204
Longwood Gardens: 200, 208
Mt. Cuba Center: 162
© Mystic Seaport Museum Collection: 30 (*American Eagle*, 1939.1564)
Courtesy of Winterthur Museum, Garden, and Library: 36, 80, 95

First published in the United States in 2023 by The Monacelli Press, a division of Phaidon Press Inc.
All rights reserved.

PAGES 2-3: Spring in Azalea Woods, Winterthur Museum, Garden, and Library.
PAGES 4-5: Reflecting Pool at Nemours Estate.
PAGES 6-7: Autumn dogwood foliage, tawny wildflowers, and warm season grasses in the meadow at Mt. Cuba Center.
PAGES 8-9: Summer display along the Flower Garden Walk at Longwood Gardens.
PAGES 10-11: Brandywine Creek and an abandoned railway siding at Hagley Museum and Library.
PAGES 12-13: Magnolia, flowering quince, and spirea in the Sundial Garden at Winterthur Museum, Garden, and Library.
PAGE 14-15: Japanese primroses and native plantings along a rill on the West Slope Path at Mt. Cuba Center.
PAGE 236-37: Pond at Mt. Cuba Center.
PAGE 239: Illuminated trees at Longwood Gardens.

Library of Congress Control Number: 2023934373
ISBN 978-158093-603-3
Design: Susi Oberhelman

Printed in China

Monacelli
A Phaidon Company
65 Bleecker Street
New York, New York 10012